Elayne Clift, MA
Editor

Women's Encounters with the Mental Health Establishment
Escaping the Yellow Wallpaper

Pre-publication
REVIEWS,
COMMENTARIES,
EVALUATIONS . . .

"In this riveting book, searing accounts of women's encounters with the mental health system reveal frank brutality and an appalling lack of compassion from the very people who are called upon to help. The failure to care, to offer even small bits of genuine contact, understanding, and kindness help to generate the pain, devastation, fear, and anger that are these women's companions as they struggle, alone, to save themselves. In Elayne Clift's newest book, the women tell their stories . . . and the world *does* split apart."

Anne S. Kasper, PhD
Author, *Breast Cancer:*
Society Shapes an Epidemic

"Elayne Clift has been courageous in shaping an anthology that documents so effectively the necessity to restructure the power dynamic still so damaging to women in the mental health system. Breaking traditional patterns of invisibility, the contributors dare to offer compelling testimonies about their experiences with the people and institutions designed to help and protect them. This book will clearly serve as a welcome companion for consumers and their families, a poignant guide for practitioners, and a call to the public about the fine line between effective and ineffective care."

Jean Gould
Co-founder, TELL
(Therapy Exploitation Link Line);
Editor, *Dutiful Daughters:*
Caring for Our Parents
As They Grow Old

More pre-publication
REVIEWS, COMMENTARIES, EVALUATIONS . . .

"*Girl, Interrupted* meets *One Flew Over the Cuckoo's Nest* in this beautifully crafted and unsettling anthology. Well-known writers and their lesser-known sisters offer heartfelt testimony—in poetry and prose—about personal encounters with the mental health system. Many of the pieces are raw and angry, and readers will come away from the text with an enhanced understanding of the infantilization and humiliation that all too often accompanies psychiatric care. Likewise, the particular indignities levied against women are spotlighted. Nonetheless, there are positive glimmers and many of the pieces showcase the process of recovery and demonstrate the beneficent intervention of compassionate professionals. Their small kindnesses offer instructive guidance for both current and aspiring mental health workers. This book should be required reading in all social work, psychology, and psychiatry training programs."

Eleanor J. Bader, MSW
Co-author, *Targets of Hatred:*
Anti-Abortion Terrorism

"*Women's Encounters with the Mental Health Establishment* is a rich collection of jewels, poetry, and brave, poetic prose written by women who have had experience with the mental health system. The contributors give us a remarkable variety of experience, perspective, and emotion about their encounters with that system, and reading their work, we are variously touched, astonished, and enraged. They portray the oft-forgotten humanity and pain of the people labeled 'mental patients' and the deeply moving humanity and help offered by some people called 'helping professionals'; but they also, importantly, show us in exquisite detail the bewilderment, shame, fear, and even devastation too many professionals bring to their patients' lives by thoughtlessly choosing treatments and by turning deaf ears to their patients' cries when the treatments make them worse. This book does us all a great service by reminding us that 'mental' patients deserve our respect, our gentleness, and our critical thinking about what really does and what really does not help any individual person among them."

Paula J. Caplan, PhD
Author, *They Say You're Crazy:*
How the World's Most Powerful
Psychiatrists Decide Who's Normal
and *The Myth of Women's Masochism*

"Elayne Clift has assembled a collection of prose and poetry that is both poignant and potent. In this valuable anthology, women narrate with sensitivity and complex insight their interactions with a mental health establishment often unable to treat them humanely. Their voices speak eloquently to women's unstoppable quest for dignity and self-respect.

As much about the power of writing to heal as about the power of women's voices to be heard, this much-needed anthology will be useful not only to mental health professionals interested in building patient-centered practices, but also to women's studies teachers and teachers of writing."

Kathleen B. Jones, PhD
Author,
Living Between Danger and Love:
The Limits of Choice;
Professor of Women's Studies,
San Diego State University

Women's Encounters with the Mental Health Establishment
Escaping the Yellow Wallpaper

THE HAWORTH PRESS
New, Recent, and Forthcoming
Titles of Related Interest

Tending Inner Gardens: The Healing Art of Psychotherapy by Lesley Irene Shore

Anorexia Nervosa and Recovery: A Hunger for Meaning by Karen Way

The Way of the Woman Writer, Second Edition by Janet Lynn Roseman

Feminist Theories and Feminist Psychotherapies: Origins, Themes, and Variations by Carolyn Zerbe Enns

Unbroken Homes: Single-Parent Mothers Tell Their Stories by Wendy A. Paterson

Women at the Margins: Neglect, Punishment, and Resistance edited by Josefina Figueira-McDonough and Rosemary C. Sarri

Women's Stories of Divorce at Childbirth: When the Baby Rocks the Cradle by Hilary Hoge

Integrating Spirit and Psyche: Using Women's Narratives in Psychotherapy by Mary Pat Henehan

Women's Best Friendships: Beyond Betty, Veronica, Thelma, and Louise by Patricia Rind

Transforming the Disciplines: A Women's Studies Primer edited by Elizabeth L. MacNabb

Women's Encounters with the Mental Health Establishment
Escaping the Yellow Wallpaper

Elayne Clift, MA
Editor

The Haworth Press®
New York • London • Oxford

The Haworth Press, Inc., 10 Alice Street, Binghamton, NY 13904-1580.

"When Therapy Works" by Maryhelen Snyder first appeared in the *Journal of Humanistic Psychology*, Vol. 40, No. 2, Spring 2000.

"Going Out" by Catherine Turnbull first appeared in *Calliope*, Vol. 16, No. 2, Spring/Summer 1993.

"Since You Asked, Here Is Why" by Amy Stuber first appeared in the *Colorado Review*, Vol. XX, No. 2, Fall 1993.

Excerpt from *Welcome to My Country* by Lauren Slater, copyright 1996 by Lauren Slater, used by permission of Random House, Inc., and Penguin UK.

Excerpt from *Undercurrents*, copyright 1995 by Martha Manning, reprinted by permission of HarperCollins Publishers, Inc.

Excerpt from *The Loony Bin Trip*, copyright 1990, 2000 by Kate Millett, reprinted by permission of Georges Borchardt, Inc. for the author.

"You, Dr. Martin" from *The Complete Poems of Anne Sexton*. Copyright © 1981 by Linda Gray Sexton and Loring Conant, Jr., Executors of the Will of Anne Sexton. Reprinted by permission of Houghton Mifflin, and Sterling Lord Literistic, Inc. All rights reserved.

Excerpt from *The Bell Jar* by Sylvia Plath, copyright 1971 by Harper & Row, Publishers, Inc., reprinted by permission of HarperCollins Publishers, Inc. and by permission of Faber & Faber, London.

"Resume," copyright 1926, 1928, renewed 1954 © 1956 by Dorothy Parker, from *The Portable Dorothy Parker* by Dorothy Parker, edited by Brendan Gill. Used by permission of Viking Penguin, a division of Penguin Putnam Inc.

Cover design by Anastasia Litwak.

Library of Congress Cataloging-in-Publication Data

Women's encounters with the mental health establishment : escaping the yellow wallpaper / Elayne Clift, editor.
   p. cm.
   Includes bibliographical references.
   ISBN 0-7890-1545-5 (alk. paper) — ISBN 0-7890-1546-3 (alk. paper)
   1. Mentally ill women—Care. 2. Women—Mental health services. 3. Chronically ill—Care. 4. Mentally ill women—Miscellanea. I. Clift, Elayne.

RC480.53 .E83 2002
362.2'082—dc21

2001051595

For Sue,
for Walter and his family,
and especially for my mother,
whose life was a metaphor for the multitudes.

CONTENTS

About the Editor   xii

Contributors   xiii

Foreword: Women As Subjects of Their Experiences   xix
Kelley L. Phillips

Acknowledgments   xxiii

Prologue: The Yellow Wallpaper   1
Charlotte Perkins Gilman

I: HOSPITALS

From *The Loony-Bin Trip*   19
Kate Millett

Life Inside   21
Mindy Lewis

Ode to Carrie White   40
Elayne Clift

From *The Bell Jar*   41
Sylvia Plath

For Love Nor Money   45
Anonymous

Since You Asked, Here Is Why   54
Amy Stuber

Death Interrupted   61
Barbara Shooltz Kendzierski

Outstanding Charges   62
Barbara Shooltz Kendzierski

The Setup   63
        Mary Hower

The Scream   75
        J. Lisa Richesson

Hospital   82
        Anne Myra Benjamin

Safe Places   86
        Catherine Ann Fabio

The Waiting Room   103
        Kathleen M. Kelley

Home Sweet Nuthouse   104
        Sara Kirschenbaum

i remember   109
        Hadiyah Carlyle

Bathing in the Bin   112
        Jo Patti

Outtakes   114
        Elayne Clift

You, Doctor Martin   118
        Anne Sexton

II: THERAPY

From *Welcome to My Country*   123
        Lauren Slater

The Caregivers' Dance   126
        Catherine Spensley

The Psychoanalyst's Daughter: A Memoir   135
        Karen Wunsch

Vested Interests   145
      Geraldine A. J. Sanford

Putdown   146
      Geraldine A. J. Sanford

Is She Really Listening?   147
      Anna Mills

We Go a Little Over the Hour   152
      Kathleen M. Kelley

Suite 506   154
      Barbara Shooltz Kendzierski

Escaping the Cabin   156
      Adrienne Ross

Therapy   164
      Celia Jeffries

Preview   166
      Nancy A. McMichael

From *Undercurrents*   170
      Martha Manning

It's Going to Be a Great Daypro   173
      Megeen R. Mulholland

Side Effects May Include: 174
      Megeen R. Mulholland

Transference   176
      Beth Schorr Jaffe

Consult   180
      Mary Damon Peltier

Why Have You Come to My Office Today?
Why Have You Come to the Hospital? 181
Mary Damon Peltier

My Last Freudian 182
Kake Huck

Fragments 183
Kake Huck

Misinterpreting Body 184
Cathleen Calbert

Dr. Abe's Psychotherapy 185
Shira Dentz

Going Out 188
Catherine Turnbull

Therapy Session 189
Sharon Carter

Just One Question Doctor—About My Termination 190
Beth Schorr Jaffe

The Story of My Therapy 192
Sondra Zeidenstein

III: HOPE

Mrs. Gould 195
Mindy Lewis

Woman Knows It's Time to Quit Therapy 200
Barbara Schmitz

Simple Prayer 201
Anonymous

Clarity 204
Janet Ruth Heller

Saying Goodbye   205
     Pamela Malone

Keeping Our Distance   207
     Lee Kottner

Carol   209
     Carol Barrett

Reflections for a Psychiatric Resident   211
     Barbara Shooltz Kendzierski

When Therapy Works   213
     Maryhelen Snyder

Afterword   215
     Wanda K. Mohr

ABOUT THE EDITOR

Elayne Clift, MA, a writer and journalist in Saxtons River, Vermont, teaches women's studies and health communication at several New England colleges and universities. A Vermont Humanities Scholar and a public member of the Vermont State Nursing Board, she is the author of several books of prose and poetry. Her articles, commentaries, and other writings have been widely published internationally.

CONTRIBUTORS

Carol Barrett holds doctorates in both clinical psychology and creative writing. She serves on the faculty of the Union Institute in Cincinnati. In 1991, she received a Creative Writing Fellowship from the National Endowment for the Arts. Her poetry appears in eighty literary magazines and fifteen anthologies.

Anne Myra Benjamin lives in Far Rockaway, New York. Reinforced by a PhD in French Literature, she is currently taking care of her husband and four children, studying Latin and Russian, teaching ESL to Russian immigrants, and completing a commentary on the Pentateuch as well as an exercise book on American idioms.

Cathleen Calbert is the author of two books of poetry: *Lessons in Space* (1997) and *Bad Judgment* (1999). Her poems have appeared in *The Pushcart Prize XXV, Poet Lore, The Paris Review, Poetry,* and *The Southern Review.* She is an associate professor at Rhode Island College.

Hadiyah Carlyle was the first woman ship welder in Bellington, Washington, in the 1970s. Now a writer in New York, she leads workshops on healing through creative expression.

Sharon Carter received her medical degree from Cambridge University, England, and immigrated in 1979. After training as a family practitioner, she became board certified in psychiatry in 1990. Her poems have been published in *Mediphors, Pandora,* and *Raven Chronicles.* She lives near Seattle.

Shira Dentz lives in Brooklyn, New York. One of her stories was a semifinalist for the Nelson Algren Award, and a finalist for the Heekin Foundation Fellowship for short fiction. Her poems have appeared in numerous publications including *13th Moon, Phoebe, Salt Hill Journal, The Evergreen Chronicles,* and *Cimarron Review.* In 1998 and 1999, she was a semifinalist in the "Discovery"/*The Nation* contest.

Catherine Ann Fabio earned a Masters degree in psychology and human development from Harvard University in 1997. She is currently a doctoral student in clinical child development. She is a member of the Radcliffe Writing Seminar where she is working on her first book, *Disentangling the Voices: A Story of Hope and Healing.*

Charlotte Perkins Gilman was born in 1860. A writer and social activist, she is best known for her short story "The Yellow Wallpaper." She also wrote the feminist utopian novel *Herland* and the 1898 classic *Women and Economics.* She died in 1935.

Janet Ruth Heller teaches English and Women's Studies courses at Western Michigan University. Her poetry has appeared in *Anima, Organic Gardening, The Writer, Lilith, Our Mothers' Daughters, Light Year, Modern Maturity,* and *Women's Glib.* She is a founding mother of *Primavera,* a women's literary magazine.

Mary Hower is a poet and fund-raiser living in San Francisco. Her poetry has appeared in numerous literary journals, including *13th Moon, Threepenny Review, Virginia Quarterly Review, Nimrod,* and *Iowa Review.* She plays the violin and is an avid gardener.

Kake Huck has won two Oregon poetry contests and her work has been accepted by *Enigma, Pearl, Bylines, Messages from the Heart,* and *Muse of Fire.* While she has been labeled manic-depressive and the owner of a schizoaffective dysfunction, she prefers to think of herself as a high-functioning loony.

Beth Schorr Jaffe is the author of a novel called *Fade to Blue.* She is currently at work on her second novel, and most recently had a story included in Simon and Schuster's *Chocolate for the Young Woman's Soul.* She lives in New Jersey with her husband and two sons.

Celia Jeffries started writing the first time she was handed a pen and paper. Over the years she has been a teacher, a reporter, and an editor. She now devotes her time to writing fiction.

Kathleen M. Kelley is a poet, psychotherapist, and medical social worker who lives in Northampton, Massachusetts. She draws from many paradigms of thought and language, including the personal, the spiritual, and the political. She is concerned with questions about the nature of connection and disconnection, ecstasy and grief, creativity, power, work, and spirituality. Her work has appeared in a variety of literary magazines and periodicals.

Barbara Shooltz Kendzierski first published her poetry at age seven (one copy for her parents). A University of Michigan Law School graduate, she enjoys reading, speaking on mental health issues, poetry, and time spent on the Great Lakes with her husband and two sons. She is co-author of *Up from the Soles of Our Feet* (Plain View Press, 1998).

Sara Kirschenbaum's essay is part of a collection in progress, *Taboo Mama*. She is a 1999 graduate of Antioch University's MFA program in creative writing. She lives on a microurban farm in Portland, Oregon, with her two children, Sage and Annie Dove.

Lee Kottner is a writer and editor living in Brooklyn, New York. Her poetry has appeared in several journals and anthologies, and in a chapbook from Blue Stone Press. She has just completed her first novel, *Prospero's Daughter,* and is working on a how-to book called *Involuntary Simplicity: How to Have a Fabulous Life on a Miserable Salary,* with Robert Kellerman.

Mindy Lewis expresses her creativity through painting and printmaking, in addition to working as a graphic designer. A native New Yorker, she writes fiction and creative nonfiction and is currently working on her first novel. Her work has been published in *Lilith*.

Pamela Malone has been writing for twenty-seven years. In that time she has published ninety-one poems, thirty short stories, and seventeen essays. She is the Associate Editor, Prose Editor, and Book Reviewer for *Wings Online Magazine*. She teaches ESL and lives in New Jersey with her husband.

Martha Manning is a writer and psychologist. She received her PhD from Catholic University in Washington, DC. Her latest book is *Chasing Amy* (1996). She also writes for such magazines as *Ladies Home Journal* and *Harper's Bazaar.*

Nancy A. McMichael is Hoosier born and influenced, and now lives, writes, and teaches in Bethlehem, Pennsylvania.

Kate Millett is a writer and artist living in New York. She is best known for her feminist classic, *Sexual Politics.*

Anna Mills teaches, writes, and dances. Her biggest realization is that heterosexism and sexism give rise to women's body image problems. She writes "to speak the unspeakable."

Megeen R. Mulholland is currently pursuing doctoral studies in English at the University at Albany, New York. Her work has appeared in *The Seattle Review, Earth's Daughters, Barkeater,* and other literary journals. Since writing the pieces included here, she has taken healing into her own hands.

Jo Patti has been published in *The Manhattan Poetry Review, Eve's Eden Anthology, The Poet, Poets On, Andrew Mountain Press,* and other journals in the United States. She was a featured performance poet at the 1999 Austin International Poetry Festival. She is a choreographer, teacher, dancer, storyteller, and "most important, a mother."

Mary Damon Peltier is a writer, gardener, and painter in New England. Her work has been published in numerous journals and anthologies. Her psychiatric adventures began after a disabling back injury. She is grateful to art therapists everywhere.

Sylvia Plath, poet and writer, lived in London when she died in 1963.

J. Lisa Richesson has been writing professionally for nearly twenty years, starting as a book reviewer for *The Seattle Times*. Her work has been published in *Women's Artist News, Girlfriends, Bathtub Gin,* and the *Seattle LRC News*. A native of Seattle, she lives with her partner and three cats.

Adrienne Ross lives in Seattle, Washington. Her work has appeared in *Tikkun, Northern Lights, New Age Journal,* and other magazines as well as in several anthologies, including the 1996, 1997, and 2000 *American Nature Writing*.

Geraldine A. J. Sanford has taught at the University of Minnesota, Morris, and the University of South Dakota, Vermillion. She served as an editor of *South Dakota Review* and has published poetry, fiction, and essays in various journals. She is the author of a poetry collection called *Unverified Sightings from Dakota East*.

Barbara Schmitz started taking herself seriously as a writer when Allen Ginsberg told her to in 1978. Her poetry collection, *How to Get Out of the Body,* was published by Sandhills Press in September 1999. She won a 1997 Nebraska Arts Council Poetry Award.

Anne Sexton was a Pulitzer Prize–winning poet. She committed suicide in October 1974.

Lauren Slater is an award-winning writer and psychologist who has written extensively about her own experiences with mental illness. A professor at Goucher College in Maryland, her latest book is *Lying: A Metaphorical Memoir* (2000).

Maryhelen Snyder resides in Albuquerque, New Mexico, where she is a practicing psychologist and family therapist, an Adjunct Professor at the University of New Mexico in the Departments of Psychology and Psychiatry, and a writer. Her published work includes two books of poems, *Enough* (Solo Press, 1979) and *Because I Praise* (Watermelon Mountain Press, 1998), an edited issue of *Cafe Solo,* an edited volume on *Ethical Issues in Feminist Family Therapy* (The Haworth Press, 1996), and chapters in several professional books.

Catherine Spensley has written screenplays for television and film and worked as a journalist, but her passion is creative writing. After living in Rome and the Caribbean, she has settled in San Francisco with her husband, two cats, and an extended family of fellow artists. She is finishing her second novel.

Amy Stuber earned her PhD from the University of Kansas and now teaches English at Haskell Indian Nations University. Her work has been published in the *Sonora Review, Kiosk,* and *Primavera.*

Catherine Turnbull is a poet who lives with her family in Interlochen, Michigan.

Karen Wunsch has published fiction and memoir in *Harper's Bazaar, Epoc, The Kansas Quarterly, The North Dakota Quarterly, Confrontation, Ascent, Event, Silo,* and numerous reviews. She teaches English at Queensborough Community College in New York.

Sondra Zeidenstein's poems have been published in magazines, journals, and anthologies, including *The Ledge, Women's Review of Books, Yellow Silk,* and *Passionate Lives* (Queen of Swords Press, 1998). Zeidenstein is publisher of Chicory Blue Press, a small literary press that focuses on writing by women past sixty.

Foreword

Women As Subjects
of Their Experiences

"The Yellow Wallpaper" in this moving anthology belongs to feminist writer and social critic Charlotte Perkins Gilman, who wrote her classic autobiographical short story about her encounter with madness and the destructive treatment of the day in 1890. The story first appeared in 1892, then reappeared in 1920 in *The Great American Short Stories,* and was again reissued in 1973 by The Feminist Press. Gilman's powerful story came to represent contemporary women's struggle to be understood by the mental health establishment. This is the major theme of this collection: women wanting to be understood by practitioners, often strangers, whom they or family members approach, at a most vulnerable time for support, hope, and wisdom.

Now you will have the opportunity to read Gilman's work, perhaps for the first time, offered as prologue to this astonishing collection of women's stories. Here, both famous and nonpublic women write about their multidimensional truths as they have encountered various mental health settings. In moving prose and in self-disclosing verse, these works speak to us about the mental health environment first-hand, often revealing its lack of woman-centered focus and an alarmingly diminished humanity.

These textured and poignant works stand as metaphor for any woman who has ever found herself without voice in the presence of those she reaches out to for help and solace.

By including her own experiences, perceptions, and memories, editor Elayne Clift is one with her contributors. In "Outtakes," she shares the raw, throbbing pain of visiting her mother in a psychiatric hospital at a formative age. Images of fear, abandonment, and violation mingle with her own sense of helplessness. When her troubled parent continues to exist in body but with tormented mind and soul, it is burdensome and depleting to be the responsible adult daughter. This experience creates a passionate voice for the daughter who now calls upon practitioners to hear our mothers, our daughters, our sisters.

Barbara Shooltz Kendzierski addresses a young physician training in psychiatry with her work, "Reflections for a Psychiatric Resident." She inspires anyone in the helping professions to feel humble. Clinicians, she admonishes, remember your awesome power to create tremendous healing or cause devastating pain. Relate to me as another human being when I come to you vulnerable and hurting. My trust in you is a privilege. Listen. Understand my story and do not assume to know. Be present with me. Perhaps then I can begin to heal.

"My Last Freudian," a poem by Kake Huck, searingly conveys a psychoanalyst's misguided attempt to use traditionally structured therapy with a frightened woman. She responds with a sea of distrust and is piqued by his arrogance. He conveys a male-dominant frame of reference. She wishes to be understood, but only by those who can hear her story.

Themes throughout these writings echo the patriarchal structure and form prevalent in most mental health institutions and practices. Clinicians continue to apply male-derived diagnoses and treatments and to ignore the reality of women's experience. This frame of reference offers a hierarchical and unidimensional perspective and the individual person is rarely recognized. Treatment is linked to disease. This is, after all, what clinicians know. Women are offered scripts, and when these scripts don't apply, they are labeled difficult, noncompliant, chronically ill.

This creative and artistic anthology is meant to destroy those stereotypes. It is a literary work for the fields of women's studies and mental health. Both moving and powerful, it offers support and affirmation for women in moments of vulnerability while providing possibilities for heightened sensitivity to women's perspectives on the part of practitioners.

Vivid descriptions of tremendous gaps in the mental health system reveal how women struggle with the new and strange therapeutic environment, so devoid of advocacy. Staff assume that the mental health milieu is appropriate for those who enter. With unwarranted arrogance, institutions and individuals apply patriarchal models that are, more often than not, wrong for women. Issues of power, trust, autonomy, sense of self, and vulnerability are major themes too often ignored in this context. Only in reciprocity is there wisdom and knowledge for all concerned.

This collection serves as a powerful textbook for those of us who work in the mental health field. We spend much time in training learning about institutional structures, what environments are safe from physical injury, medications to treat diagnoses rather than people, and therapies to offer support and insights into a painful personal world. But our methods are usually offered from the perspective of clinicians and scientists who capture at best one or two dimensions of an individual. We often lose the real person with these approaches. We measure what we know how to measure, not what is. We attempt to offer empathy, skills, and techniques to assist with healing for those who seek our help. Yet, the current environment, structure, and discourse are often not conducive to women's healing. The facts seem clear enough. We do not explore well-being. We know a little about disease but not much about women and the reality of their lives. We lose sight of humanity. We cling to a duality of mind and body and thus we miss the complex, multidimensional person altogether.

Practitioners often do not adequately address severe side effects of powerful drugs that leave one with cottony thinking, transformed body image, and slowed reflexes. Women mourn these effects, which are experienced as giving up part of oneself and one's autonomy. Women who have recovered and can tell their stories to those who follow are the best mentors to assuage the frightening images of lifeless rooms, ugly corridors, and institutional garb in a surreal world.

Reading these powerful stories reminds us of our need to integrate the context, history, and experience of any woman with whom we work. As mental health professionals, we are part of her context. We bring our own history, experience, and worldviews to the relationship between woman and practitioner. Context is personal and multidimensional. We must learn to respect it. Trust, dignity, and power issues are palpable and must be addressed in any meaningful, healing relationship.

This collection of works is also meant for women who access the mental health milieu and experience their encounters as alien, isolating, and pejorative. You are not alone. Take this book with you.

Kelley L. Phillips, MD, MPH
President, American College
of Women's Health Physicians
and the Foundation for Women's Health

Acknowledgments

I am deeply indebted to all the women who shared their stories with me, including those whose work does not appear in this anthology. Their honesty only serves to ease the way for others. I wish to thank Deborah Fort for her experienced and gentle editorial eye, Kelley Phillips and Wanda Mohr for their sensitive and insightful "bookends" to this work, and Bill Palmer and his team at The Haworth Press for recognizing the importance of this collection and for being so easy to work with.

Prologue

The Yellow Wallpaper

Charlotte Perkins Gilman

It is very seldom that mere ordinary people like John and myself secure ancestral halls for the summer.

A colonial mansion, a hereditary estate, I would say a haunted house, and reach the height of romantic felicity—but that would be asking too much of fate!

Still I will proudly declare that there is something queer about it.

Else, why should it be let so cheaply? And why have stood so long untenanted?

John laughs at me, of course, but one expects that in marriage.

John is practical in the extreme. He has no patience with faith, an intense horror of superstition, and he scoffs openly at any talk of things not to be felt and seen and put down in figures.

John is a physician, and *perhaps*—(I would not say it to a living soul, of course, but this is dead paper and a great relief to my mind)—*perhaps* that is one reason I do not get well faster.

You see, he does not believe I am sick!

And what can one do?

If a physician of high standing, and one's own husband, assures friends and relatives that there is really nothing the matter with one but temporary nervous depression—a slight hysterical tendency—what is one to do?

My brother is also a physician, and also of high standing, and he says the same thing.

So I take phosphates or phosphites—whichever it is—and tonics, and journeys, and air, and exercise, and am absolutely forbidden to "work" until I am well again.

From *New England Magazine,* January 1892.

Personally, I disagree with their ideas.

Personally, I believe that congenial work, with excitement and change, would do me good.

But what is one to do?

I did write for a while in spite of them; but it *does* exhaust me a good deal—having to be so sly about it, or else meet with heavy opposition.

I sometimes fancy that in my condition if I had less opposition and more society and stimulus—but John says the very worst thing I can do is to think about my condition, and I confess it always makes me feel bad.

So I will let it alone and talk about the house.

The most beautiful place! It is quite alone, standing well back from the road, quite three miles from the village. It makes me think of English places that you read about, for there are hedges and walls and gates that lock, and lots of separate little houses for the gardeners and people.

There is a *delicious* garden! I never saw such a garden—large and shady, full of box-bordered paths, and lined with long grape-covered arbors with seats under them.

There were greenhouses, too, but they are all broken now.

There was some legal trouble, I believe, something about the heirs and coheirs; anyhow, the place has been empty for years.

That spoils my ghostliness, I am afraid, but I don't care—there is something strange about the house—I can feel it.

I even said so to John one moonlight evening, but he said what I felt was a *draught,* and shut the window.

I get unreasonably angry with John sometimes. I'm sure I never used to be so sensitive. I think it is due to this nervous condition.

But John says if I feel so, I shall neglect proper self-control; so I take pains to control myself—before him, at least, and that makes me very tired.

I don't like our room a bit. I wanted one downstairs that opened on the piazza and had roses all over the window, and such pretty old-fashioned chintz hangings! But John would not hear of it.

He said there was only one window and not room for two beds, and no near room for him if he took another.

He is very careful and loving, and hardly lets me stir without special direction.

I have a schedule prescription for each hour in the day; he takes all care from me, and so I feel basely ungrateful not to value it more.

He said we came here solely on my account, that I was to have perfect rest and all the air I could get. "Your exercise depends on your strength, my dear," said he, "and your food somewhat on your appetite; but air you can absorb all the time." So we took the nursery at the top of the house.

It is a big, airy room, the whole floor nearly, with windows that look all ways, and air and sunshine galore. It was nursery first and then playroom and gymnasium, I should judge; for the windows are barred for little children, and there are rings and things in the walls.

The paint and paper look as if a boys' school had used it. It is stripped off—the paper—in great patches all around the head of my bed, about as far as I can reach, and in a great place on the other side of the room low down. I never saw a worse paper in my life.

One of those sprawling, flamboyant patterns committing every artistic sin.

It is dull enough to confuse the eye in following, pronounced enough to constantly irritate and provoke study, and when you follow the lame uncertain curves for a little distance they suddenly commit suicide—plunge off at outrageous angles, destroy themselves in unheard-of contradictions.

The color is repellent, almost revolting: a smouldering unclean yellow, strangely faded by the slow-turning sunlight.

It is a dull yet lurid orange in some places, a sickly sulphur tint in others.

No wonder the children hated it! I should hate it myself if I had to live in this room long.

There comes John, and I must put this away—he hates to have me write a word.

We have been here two weeks, and I haven't felt like writing before, since that first day.

I am sitting by the window now, up in this atrocious nursery, and there is nothing to hinder my writing as much as I please, save lack of strength.

John is away all day, and even some nights when his cases are serious.

I am glad my case is not serious!

But these nervous troubles are dreadfully depressing.

John does not know how much I really suffer. He knows there is no *reason* to suffer, and that satisfies him.

Of course it is only nervousness. It does weigh on me so not to do my duty in any way!

I meant to be such a help to John, such a real rest and comfort, and here I am a comparative burden already!

Nobody would believe what an effort it is to do what little I am able—to dress and entertain, and order things.

It is fortunate Mary is so good with the baby. Such a dear baby!

And yet I *cannot* be with him, it makes me so nervous.

I suppose John never was nervous in his life. He laughs at me so about this wallpaper!

At first he meant to repaper the room, but afterwards he said that I was letting it get the better of me, and that nothing was worse for a nervous patient than to give way to such fancies.

He said that after the wallpaper was changed it would be the heavy bedstead, and then the barred windows, and then that gate at the head of the stairs, and so on.

"You know the place is doing you good," he said, "and really, dear, I don't care to renovate the house just for a three months' rental."

"Then do let us go downstairs," I said. "There are such pretty rooms there."

Then he took me in his arms and called me a blessed little goose, and said he would go down to the cellar, if I wished, and have it white-washed into the bargain.

But he is right enough about the beds and windows and things.

It is as airy and comfortable a room as anyone need wish, and, of course, I would not be so silly as to make him uncomfortable just for a whim.

I'm really getting quite fond of the big room, all but that horrid paper.

Out of one window I can see the garden, those mysterious deep-shaded arbors, the riotous old-fashioned flowers, and bushes and gnarly trees.

Out of another I get a lovely view of the bay and a little private wharf belonging to the estate. There is a beautiful shaded lane that runs down there from the house. I always fancy I see people walking in these numerous paths and arbors, but John has cautioned me not to give way to fancy in the least. He says that with my imaginative power and habit of story-making, a nervous weakness like mine is sure to lead to all manner of excited fancies, and that I ought to use my will and good sense to check the tendency. So I try.

I think sometimes that if I were only well enough to write a little it would relieve the press of ideas and rest me.

But I find I get pretty tired when I try.

It is so discouraging not to have any advice and companionship about my work. When I get really well, John says we will ask Cousin Henry and Julia down for a long visit; but he says he would as soon put fireworks in my pillow-case as to let me have those stimulating people about now.

I wish I could get well faster.

But I must not think about that. This paper looks to me as if it *knew* what a vicious influence it had!

There is a recurrent spot where the pattern lolls like a broken neck and two bulbous eyes stare at you upside down.

I get positively angry with the impertinence of it and the everlastingness. Up and down and sideways they crawl, and those absurd, unblinking eyes are everywhere. There is one place where two breadths didn't match, and the eyes go all up and down the line, one a little higher than the other.

I never saw so much expression in an inanimate thing before, and we all know how much expression they have! I used to lie awake as a child and get more entertainment and terror out of blank walls and plain furniture than most children could find in a toy-store.

I remember what a kindly wink the knobs of our big, old bureau used to have, and there was one chair that always seemed like a strong friend.

I used to feel that if any of the other things looked too fierce I could always hop into that chair and be safe.

The furniture in this room is no worse than inharmonious, however, for we had to bring it all from downstairs. I suppose when this was used as a playroom they had to take the nursery things out, and no wonder! I never saw such ravages as the children have made here.

The wallpaper, as I said before, is torn off in spots, and it sticketh closer than a brother—they must have had perseverance as well as hatred.

Then the floor is scratched and gouged and splintered, the plaster itself is dug out here and there, and this great heavy bed, which is all we found in the room, looks as if it had been through the wars.

But I don't mind it a bit—only the paper.

There comes John's sister. Such a dear girl as she is, and so careful of me! I must not let her find me writing.

She is a perfect and enthusiastic housekeeper, and hopes for no better profession. I verily believe she thinks it is the writing which made me sick!

But I can write when she is out, and see her a long way off from these windows.

There is one that commands the road, a lovely shaded winding road, and one that just looks off over the country. A lovely country, too, full of great elms and velvet meadows.

This wallpaper has a kind of sub-pattern in a different shade, a particularly irritating one, for you can only see it in certain lights, and not clearly then.

But in the places where it isn't faded and where the sun is just so—I can see a strange, provoking, formless, sort of figure that seems to skulk about behind that silly and conspicuous front design.

There's sister on the stairs!

Well, the Fourth of July is over! The people are all gone, and I am tired out. John thought it might do me good to see a little company, so we just had Mother and Nellie and the children down for a week.

Of course I didn't do a thing. Jennie sees to everything now.

But it tired me all the same.

John says if I don't pick up faster he shall send me to Weir Mitchell in the fall.

But I don't want to go there at all. I had a friend who was in his hands once, and she says he is just like John and my brother, only more so!

Besides, it is such an undertaking to go so far.

I don't feel as if it was worthwhile to turn my hand over for anything, and I'm getting dreadfully fretful and querulous.

I cry at nothing, and cry most of the time.

Of course I don't when John is here, or anybody else, but when I am alone.

And I am alone a good deal just now. John is kept in town very often by serious cases, and Jennie is good and lets me alone when I want her to.

So I walk a little in the garden or down that lovely lane, sit on the porch under the roses, and lie down up here a good deal.

I'm getting really fond of the room in spite of the wallpaper. Perhaps *because* of the wallpaper.

It dwells in my mind so!

I lie here on this great immovable bed—it is nailed down, I believe—and follow that pattern about by the hour. It is as good as gymnastics, I assure you. I start, we'll say, at the bottom, down in the corner over there where it has not been touched, and I determine for the thousandth time that I *will* follow that pointless pattern to some sort of a conclusion.

I know a little of the principle of design, and I know this thing was not arranged on any laws of radiation, or alternation, or repetition, or symmetry, or anything else that I have ever heard of.

It is repeated, of course, by the breadths, but not otherwise.

Looked at in one way each breadth stands alone, the bloated curves and flourishes—a kind of "debased Romanesque" with *delirium tremens*—go waddling up and down in isolated columns of fatuity.

But, on the other hand, they connect diagonally, and the sprawling outlines run off in great slanting waves of optic horror, like a lot of wallowing seaweeds in full chase.

The whole thing goes horizontally, too, at least it seems so, and I exhaust myself trying to distinguish the order of its going in that direction.

They have a horizontal breadth for a frieze, and that adds wonderfully to the confusion.

There is one end of the room where it is almost intact, and there, when the crosslights fade and the low sun shines directly upon it, I can almost fancy radiation after all—the interminable grotesques seem to form around a common center and rush off in headlong plunges of equal distraction.

It makes me tired to follow it. I will take a nap I guess.

I don't know why I should write this.

I don't want to.

I don't feel able.

And I know John would think it absurd. But I *must* say what I feel and think in some way—it is such a relief!

But the effort is getting to be greater than the relief.

Half the time now I am awfully lazy, and lie down ever so much.

John says I mustn't lose my strength, and has me take cod liver oil and lots of tonics and things, to say nothing of ale and wine and rare meat.

Dear John! He loves me very dearly, and hates to have me sick. I tried to have a real earnest reasonable talk with him the other day, and tell him how I wish he would let me go and make a visit to Cousin Henry and Julia.

But he said I wasn't able to go, nor able to stand it after I got there; and I did not make out a very good case for myself, for I was crying before I had finished.

It is getting to be a great effort for me to think straight. Just this nervous weakness I suppose.

And dear John gathered me up in his arms, and just carried me upstairs and laid me on the bed, and sat by me and read to me till it tired my head.

He said I was his darling and his comfort and all he had, and that I must take care of myself for his sake, and keep well.

He says no one but myself can help me out of it, that I must use my will and self-control and not let any silly fancies run away with me.

There's one comfort, the baby is well and happy, and does not have to occupy this nursery with the horrid wallpaper.

If we had not used it, that blessed child would have! What a fortunate escape! Why, I wouldn't have a child of mine, an impressionable little thing, live in such a room for worlds.

I never thought of it before, but it is lucky that John kept me here after all, I can stand it so much easier than a baby, you see.

Of course I never mention it to them any more—I am too wise—but I keep watch of it all the same.

There are things in that wallpaper that nobody knows but me, or ever will.

Behind that outside pattern the dim shapes get clearer every day.

It is always the same shape, only very numerous. And it is like a woman stooping down and creeping about behind that pattern. I don't like it a bit. I wonder—I begin to think—I wish John would take me away from here!

It is so hard to talk with John about my case, because he is so wise, and because he loves me so.

But I tried it last night.

It was moonlight. The moon shines in all around just as the sun does.

I hate to see it sometimes, it creeps so slowly, and always comes in by one window or another.

John was asleep and I hated to waken him, so I kept still and watched the moonlight on that undulating wallpaper till I felt creepy.

The faint figure behind seemed to shake the pattern, just as if she wanted to get out.

I got up softly and went to feel and see if the paper *did* move, and when I came back John was awake.

"What is it, little girl?" he said. "Don't go walking about like that—you'll get cold."

I thought it was a good time to talk, so I told him that I really was not gaining here, and that I wished he would take me away.

"Why, darling!" said he, "our lease will be up in three weeks, and I can't see how to leave before.

"The repairs are not done at home, and I cannot possibly leave town just now. Of course if you were in any danger, I could and would, but you really are better, dear, whether you can see it or not. I am a doctor, dear, and I know. You are gaining flesh and color, your appetite is better, I feel really much easier about you."

"I don't weigh a bit more," said I, "nor as much; and my appetite may be better in the evening when you are here, but it is worse in the morning when you are away!"

"Bless her little heart!" said he with a big hug, "she shall be as sick as she pleases! But now let's improve the shining hours by going to sleep, and talk about it in the morning!"

"And you won't go away?" I asked gloomily.

"Why, how can I, dear? It is only three weeks more and then we will take a nice little trip of a few days while Jennie is getting the house ready. Really, dear, you are better!"

"Better in body perhaps—" I began, and stopped short, for he sat up straight and looked at me with such a stern, reproachful look that I could not say another word.

"My darling," said he, "I beg of you, for my sake and for our child's sake, as well as for your own, that you will never for one instant let that idea enter your mind! There is nothing so dangerous, so fascinating, to a temperament like yours. It is a false and foolish fancy. Can you not trust me as a physician when I tell you so?"

So of course I said no more on that score, and we went to sleep before long. He thought I was asleep first, but I wasn't, and lay there for hours trying to decide whether that front pattern and the back pattern really did move together or separately.

On a pattern like this, by daylight, there is a lack of sequence, a defiance of law, that is a constant irritant to a normal mind.

The color is hideous enough, and unreliable enough, but the pattern is torturing.

You think you have mastered it, but just as you get well underway in following, it turns a back-somersault and there you are. It slaps you in the face, knocks you down, and tramples upon you. It is like a bad dream.

The outside pattern is a florid arabesque, reminding one of a fungus. If you can imagine a toadstool in joints, an interminable string of toadstools, budding and sprouting in endless convolutions—why, that is something like it.

That is, sometimes!

There is one marked peculiarity about this paper, a thing nobody seems to notice but myself, and that is that it changes as the light changes.

When the sun shoots in through the east window—I always watch for that first long, straight ray—it changes so quickly that I never can quite believe it.

That is why I watch it always.

By moonlight—the moon shines in all night when there is a moon—I wouldn't know it was the same paper.

At night in any kind of light, in twilight, candle light, lamplight, and worst of all by moonlight, it becomes bars! The outside pattern, I mean, and the woman behind it is as plain as can be.

I didn't realize for a long time what the thing was that showed behind, that dim sub-pattern, but now I am quite sure it is a woman.

By daylight she is subdued, quiet. I fancy it is the pattern that keeps her so still. It is so puzzling. It keeps me quiet by the hour.

I lie down ever so much now. John says it is good for me, and to sleep all I can.

Indeed he started the habit of making me lie down for an hour after each meal.

It is a very bad habit, I am convinced, for you see I don't sleep.

And that cultivates deceit, for I don't tell them I'm awake—oh, no!

The fact is I am getting a little afraid of John.

He seems very queer sometimes, and even Jennie has an inexplicable look.

It strikes me occasionally, just as a scientific hypothesis—that perhaps it is the paper.

I have watched John when he did not know I was looking, and come into the room suddenly on the most innocent excuses, and I've caught him several times *looking at the paper!* And Jennie too. I caught Jennie with her hand on it once.

She didn't know I was in the room and when I asked her in a quiet, a very quiet voice, with the most restrained manner possible, what she was doing with the paper—she turned around as if she had been caught stealing, and looked quite angry—asked me why I should frighten her so!

Then she said that the paper stained everything it touched, that she had found yellow smooches on all my clothes and John's, and she wished we would be more careful!

Did not that sound innocent? But I know she was studying that pattern, and I am determined that nobody shall find it out but myself.

Life is very much more exciting now than it used to be. You see I have something more to expect, to look forward to, to watch. I really do eat better, and am more quiet than I was.

John is so pleased to see me improve! He laughed a little the other day, and said I seemed to be flourishing in spite of my wallpaper.

I turned it off with a laugh. I had no intention of telling him it was *because* of the wallpaper—he would make fun of me. He might even want to take me away.

I don't want to leave now until I have found it out. There is a week more, and I think that will be enough.

I'm feeling ever so much better! I don't sleep much at night, for it is so interesting to watch developments; but I sleep a good deal in the daytime.

In the daytime it is tiresome and perplexing.

There are always new shoots on the fungus, and new shades of yellow all over it. I cannot keep count of them, though I have tried conscientiously.

It is the strangest yellow, that wallpaper! It makes me think of all the yellow things I ever saw—not beautiful ones like buttercups, but old, foul, bad yellow things.

But there is something else about that paper—the smell! I noticed it the moment we came into the room, but with so much air and sun it was not bad. Now we have had a week of fog and rain, and whether the windows are open or not, the smell is here.

It creeps all over the house.

I find it hovering in the dining-room, skulking in the parlor, hiding in the hall, lying in wait for me on the stairs.

It gets into my hair.

Even when I go to ride, if I turn my head suddenly and surprise it—there is that smell!

Such a peculiar odor, too! I have spent hours in trying to analyze it, to find what it smelled like.

It is not bad—at first—and very gentle, but quite the subtlest, most enduring odor I ever met.

In this damp weather it is awful, I wake up in the night and find it hanging over me.

It used to disturb me at first. I thought seriously of burning the house—to reach the smell.

But now I am used to it. The only thing I can think of that it is like is the *color* of the paper! A yellow smell.

There is a very funny mark on this wall, low down, near the mopboard. A streak that runs round the room. It goes behind every piece of furniture, except the bed, a long, straight, even *smooch*, as if it had been rubbed over and over.

I wonder how it was done and who did it, and what they did it for. Round and round and round—round and round and round—it makes me dizzy!

I really have discovered something at last.

Through watching so much at night, when it changes so, I have finally found out.

The front pattern *does* move—and no wonder! The woman behind shakes it!

Sometimes I think there are a great many women behind, and sometimes only one, and she crawls around fast, and her crawling shakes it all over.

Then in the very bright spots she keeps still, and in the very shady spots she just takes hold of the bars and shakes them hard.

And she is all the time trying to climb through. But nobody could climb through that pattern—it strangles so; I think that is why it has so many heads.

They get through, and then the pattern strangles them off and turns them upside down, and makes their eyes white!

If those heads were covered or taken off it would not be half so bad.

I think that woman gets out in the daytime!

And I'll tell you why—privately—I've seen her!

I can see her out of every one of my windows!

It is the same woman, I know, for she is always creeping, and most women do not creep by daylight.

I see her in that long shaded lane, creeping up and down. I see her in those dark grape arbors, creeping all around the garden.

I see her on that long road under the trees, creeping along, and when a carriage comes she hides under the blackberry vines.

I don't blame her a bit. It must be very humiliating to be caught creeping by daylight!

I always lock the door when I creep by daylight. I can't do it at night, for I know John would suspect something at once.

And John is so queer now, that I don't want to irritate him. I wish he would take another room! Besides, I don't want anybody to let that woman out at night but myself.

I often wonder if I could see her out of all the windows at once.

But, turn as fast as I can, I can only see out of one at one time.

And though I always see her, she *may* be able to creep faster than I can turn!

I have watched her sometimes away off in the open country, creeping as fast as a cloud shadow in a high wind.

If only that top pattern could be gotten off from the under one! I mean to try it, little by little.

I have found out another funny thing, but I shan't tell it this time! It does not do to trust people too much.

There are only two more days to get this paper off, and I believe John is beginning to notice. I don't like the look in his eyes.

And I heard him ask Jennie a lot of professional questions about me. She had a very good report to give.

She said I slept a good deal in the daytime.

John knows I don't sleep very well at night, for all I'm so quiet!

He asked me all sorts of questions, too, and pretended to be very loving and kind.

As if I couldn't see through him!

Still, I don't wonder he acts so, sleeping under this paper for three months.

It only interests me, but I feel sure John and Jennie are secretly affected by it.

Hurrah! This is the last day, but it is enough. John is to stay in town over night, and won't be out until this evening.

Jennie wanted to sleep with me—the sly thing! But I told her I should undoubtedly rest better for a night all alone.

That was clever, for really I wasn't alone a bit! As soon as it was moonlight and that poor thing began to crawl and shake the pattern, I got up and ran to help her.

I pulled and she shook, I shook and she pulled, and before morning we had peeled off yards of that paper.

A strip about as high as my head and half around the room.

And then when the sun came and that awful pattern began to laugh at me, I declared I would finish it to-day!

We go away to-morrow, and they are moving all my furniture down again to leave things as they were before.

Jennie looked at the wall in amazement, but I told her merrily that I did it out of pure spite at the vicious thing.

She laughed and said she wouldn't mind doing it herself, but I must not get tired.

How she betrayed herself that time!

But I am here, and no person touches this paper but me—not *alive!*

She tried to get me out of the room—it was too patent! But I said it was so quiet and empty and clean now that I believed I would lie down again and sleep all I could, and not to wake me even for dinner—I would call when I woke.

So now she is gone, and the servants are gone, and the things are gone, and there is nothing left but that great bedstead nailed down, with the canvas mattress we found on it.

We shall sleep downstairs to-night, and take the boat home tomorrow.

I quite enjoy the room, now it is bare again.

How those children did tear about here!

This bedstead is fairly gnawed!

But I must get to work.

I have locked the door and thrown the key down into the front path.

I don't want to go out, and I don't want to have anybody come in, till John comes.

I want to astonish him.

I've got a rope up here that even Jennie did not find. If that woman does get out, and tries to get away, I can tie her!

But I forgot I could not reach far without anything to stand on!

This bed will *not* move!

I tried to lift and push it until I was lame, and then I got so angry I bit off a little piece at one corner—but it hurt my teeth.

Then I peeled off all the paper I could reach standing on the floor. It sticks horribly and the pattern just enjoys it! All those strangled heads and bulbous eyes and waddling fungus growths just shriek with derision!

I am getting angry enough to do something desperate. To jump out of the window would be admirable exercise, but the bars are too strong even to try.

Besides I wouldn't do it. Of course not. I know well enough that a step like that is improper and might be misconstrued.

I don't like to *look* out of the windows even—there are so many of those creeping women, and they creep so fast.

I wonder if they all come out of that wallpaper as I did?

But I am securely fastened now by my well-hidden rope—you don't get *me* out in the road there!

I suppose I shall have to get back behind the pattern when it comes night, and that is hard!

It is so pleasant to be out in this great room and creep around as I please!

I don't want to go outside. I won't, even if Jennie asks me to.

For outside you have to creep on the ground, and everything is green instead of yellow.

But here I can creep smoothly on the floor, and my shoulder just fits in that long smooch around the wall, so I cannot lose my way.

Why there's John at the door!

It is no use, young man, you can't open it!

How he does call and pound!

Now he's crying to Jennie for an axe.

It would be a shame to break down that beautiful door!

"John, dear!" said I in the gentlest voice, "the key is down by the front steps, under a plantain leaf!"

That silenced him for a few moments.

Then he said, very quietly indeed, "Open the door, my darling!"

"I can't," said I. "The key is down by the front door under a plantain leaf!"

And then I said it again, several times, very gently and slowly, and said it so often that he had to go and see, and he got it of course, and came in. He stopped short by the door.

"What is the matter?" he cried. "For God's sake, what are you doing!"

I kept on creeping just the same, but I looked at him over my shoulder.

"I've got out at last," said I, "in spite of you and Jennie. And I've pulled off most of the paper, so you can't put me back!"

Now why should that man have fainted? But he did, and right across my path by the wall, so that I had to creep over him every time!

I: HOSPITALS

From *The Loony-Bin Trip*

Kate Millett

You accommodate, you learn what to avoid, whom to placate. And the pull to be solid with the oppressed, the moral imperative toward solidarity, meets the pull toward making yourself agreeable with the guards. Yesterday I discovered that there is a little kitchen available to the patients who wash dishes. The staff kitchen really, but if you are good and smile a great deal and are very pleasant, there is real coffee there. This must be the coffee they gave me the first night—when was it? How long?—you must know; you must always know the date. You must count the days and keep a record in your night table. If you no longer know how long you have been held, how long you have been imprisoned, how will you ever get out or help yourself? What will you say when you are asked? Suppose that help came and you were unable to tell them when you were taken, the day of your arrest—it would dissolve all this horror into nothing. Forget it—make up to this bully of a nurse and admire the coffee, the glass jar of instant coffee. Would she make me some? Would she really? Or could I make it myself? Oh, I'd love to. "You can come here again if you are good." "But sure I am always good": the brogue to amuse them. "Ah, but ya take walks now, don't ya, Katherine?" "Nothing but a wee small walk it was," this with the grin of an eight-year-old. "And a great mistake it was, too," I add, perfectly serious, swallowing my own meaning while they take theirs.

If I keep this up, do I get a phone call? No, that is doctor's orders, they say. And they seem to be leveling with me. It is the doctor who has decided I will speak to no one, write to no one. Then how can I make anything happen—just wait for D'arcy? They will go on frustrating her at every turn. The system is huge, a nationwide bureaucracy. And maybe she is unable to interest anyone else. Then, too, she is busy with the women at Armagh, and she lives way out in the bog without a car and has damn little money. Maybe she has come to the end of her road, too. So the only thing I can do here is try to talk to one of the doctors. But they are never here. If one draws your blood he does not speak. If you meet one in the hall, he isn't yours or he cannot talk to you now; you are to see the nurse, who tells you to see the doctor. You are to remain on your course of medicine and try to guess how long or how much Thorazine and Prolixin and even relatively harmless and familiar old lithium. Lithium is called Pryabil here—I invariably think of a little bird having its beak jammed open. Many of the drugs here have different names, so it takes a long while to figure out which is which. And Prolixin is still a mystery to me. How does it produce the sores on Margaret's back? Why on earth prescribe something with these physical side effects? Or such psychic trauma, nightmares like mine?

There is shock always in the background. Enid has it. Delores has had it since she was eighteen; she is thirty-five now. The last time she was out she found a young man to marry. Then he jilted her, and they put her on shock again. Perhaps permanently or perhaps she will get out after a year or two, fall away and be captured again, and back to the empty look and the tremor, the blank fright of her presence in the dayroom. A beaten creature, a lifelong patient without a shred of self-confidence left. They have consumed her human substance utterly. It is painful to look at her, acutely embarrassing. To see the fear in her eyes makes one ashamed, near tears, as before some terrible malformation. You count your blessings: They don't give you shock. You have even discovered coffee. You are learning to make yourself agreeable when you forswear your vow never to speak to the staff, only the patients. The mechanics of a concentration camp and the little payoffs. Cushy it is, soft. Got your smokes and the telly, a bit to read in the papers. If you are feeling responsible you can think of someone else to address with your little toilet paper missives.

Life Inside

Mindy Lewis

"Mindy was always a well-behaved child, but lately she's stopped performing," my mother says. She addresses this remark to a small group of psychiatrists. As my mother pronounces this last word—*performing*—I stiffen in my chair. Does she think I'm some sort of puppet or doll? Clown would be more like it, dressed as I am in yellow hospital pajamas a couple of sizes too large.

It is December 6, 1967, three months before my sixteenth birthday—the date of my admission to the New York State Psychiatric Institute. This is a teaching hospital, better than most state institutions. I will be part of a community of others like me: troubled kids from middle-class backgrounds, unable to cope well enough to continue to live with their families.

It's been a downward spiral from compliant child to angry adolescent: early drug use, truancy, the tip of a lit cigarette held for a moment against my skin. Unanswerable questions clog my mind, keeping me awake at night, silencing me to near muteness. The hospital has agreed to accept me on one condition: that my mother brings me to family court and presses charges against me, placing me on court remand, making me a ward of the state—so my mother, in a moment of weakness, will not have the power to sign me out. There I will remain until they decide to discharge me, or until I turn eighteen, whichever comes first.

"She could be here as little as six months," one of the psychiatrists reassures my mother.

My heart pounds defiantly, each beat the slamming of a closing door. I had seen the impending date of my admission as a sort of token of a battle won; a badge of victory in my rebellion against my mother, a final act of defiance. It never occurs to me that I will have to live, as usual, through each day.

*   *   *

The Institute is built into the side of a cliff along Riverside Drive. The main entrance is on the tenth floor; to arrive on the fifth floor ward, you must *descend*. We live underground, nestled into rock; on one side locked windows overlook the Hudson, on the other, a wall of stone. Up to thirty men and thirty women live on one floor divided into two mirror-image halves. On each side long hallways connect two dorms, five private rooms, a bathroom, a shower room, a utility room, a locker room, a quiet room, a nurse's station. In the center is a sitting area, kitchen and dining room, elevator and locked staircase, and two living rooms which house TVs, a ping pong table, and heavy, padded chairs and couches. Beds line the dorms in neat rows, beside each one a dresser with only a few personal possessions allowed on top: books, toiletries. Here and there stuffed animals nestle atop hospital bedspreads.

I live here for twenty-seven months. It will be months before I am allowed to make a phone call, wear my own clothes, or have visitors other than my family.

*   *   *

We wake and are escorted to the bathroom. I avoid looking at my reflection in the long metal mirror above the row of sinks. Depending on your status, you may or may not close the stall door when using the toilet. If you are on observation an aide or nurse holds the door open. Showers by permission only, accompanied by staff, especially if shaving.

We line up for breakfast, do the patient shuffle. It is a hard time, between sleep and meds, a kind of limbo within limbo. Those of us on observation wear pajamas. Others wear street clothes—clothing privileges, they call it—but I haven't earned them yet. I try to make myself look attractive in my baggy pj's. *"Fea!"* the Spanish-speaking maintenance crew say to me as I pass. They must hate us for being privileged and spoiled, for being fed without laboring, for having and abusing everything they work for. Every day they clean up our mess, buffing away the spills and scuffs, bringing the linoleum to a dull sheen.

After breakfast we line up for meds outside the nurse's station. With its large windows, it is a glassy eye always watching. Inside, nurses wearing white uniforms look up at us as they write in our charts. The head nurse emerges pushing a metal cart on which jiggle bottles of pills. She hands us our morning dose—tiny white pills, round red ones, blue ovals—that rattle in little paper cups as we toss them into our mouths, washing them down with water poured carefully from a metal pitcher. Our mouths are checked for pill retention, our names checked off the list. Patients who resist or have trouble swallowing get liquid meds, clear or gem-colored cocktails that burn as they go down. If you refuse, you get an injection.

Medication is the rule, the burning absolution. Sometimes people demand more medication between times, begging for it tearfully. I resist, hiding the pills in my cheek, under my tongue. I find it odd that, objecting to my personal drug use, they are so dedicated to pumping me full of their drugs. *Let them have a taste of their own medicine,* I pray, wishing the doctors a forced experience of the flatness, distortion, and lack of luster. The nurse shines a flashlight in my mouth, probes with a wooden stick. My body turns leaden, my mind hums numbly. Objects sprout halos. I am on Thorazine, the standard-issue drug for psychosis.

Before I was admitted to P.I., the psychiatrist I'd been seeing had told me I was "phobic." That made sense; I was afraid of crowds, heights, loud noises, people. Here, I am suddenly catapulted into a new category, officially diagnosed as Schizophrenic. Somewhere I know that I am not—that I am just an angry kid, rebellious and self-destructive; but having an active imagination and little else to do, I comply. I've read *I Never Promised You a Rose Garden;* I've seen *David and Lisa.* The dramatic syntax of madness appeals to my creative side. This is the language of my new realm—I might as well add my own symptoms to the collective pot, earn the right to be called crazy, have something new to report in therapy sessions. *You want crazy; I'll give you crazy,* I vow.

After breakfast and meds there is a brief period of bustling energy as the ward divides into those going to activities and those who will stick around. The mood shifts from the cacophonic tuning-up of an orchestra to the quiet concentration of a poker game as those left behind settle into chairs in the common area. Soon you can hear the humming of the electric clock, the tap tap of cigarettes on ashtrays, the rustling of pages.

I look around at my new community. Aside from those wearing pajamas, they could be a random group of commuters awaiting their train . . . except for the motionless man staring, mouth open, dribbling a little. And maybe the twitchy woman, wrinkling and releasing her face every few seconds. Some of the patients I already know. Liz, in her twenties, pulls her bathrobe tight around her ample form and settles into a chair to read. Nancy, a talented painter, is equally talented at defying gravity. Following a leap from a bridge, they found her floating downstream. Next time, she jumped from a neighborhood roof. Pink scar tissue dots her back where she was stitched up, put back together.

We sit and wait. The hands of the clock sweep the seconds slowly. The silence buzzes, the air is heavy; medication makes it heavier. We wait, we pace, we jiggle our legs. We wait for meals, for meds, for appointments with doctors and social workers; to be escorted to the bathroom, to school, to OT and PT; for lunch, after which we go back to the dorm for a nap. We wait for sleep. Mostly we wait to get out of here. Some wait to exit more completely. Like the man who every few minutes slides from his chair to the floor, thinking he is committing suicide. He brightens briefly after shock therapy, until the next depression nails him.

Soon it will be lunchtime. In the half hour before the bell is rung, we glance at clocks and watches restlessly. Then the bell! We shuffle forward, line up, try to fathom the day's fare posted on the chalkboard. High in carbs, low in fiber, this food nourishes neither body nor spirit. I grow fat and constipated on macaroni and cheese, powdered mashed potatoes, canned vegetables, spaghetti and meatballs, cake and pudding. But when that Pavlovian bell rings, like everyone else, I salivate. What else is there to do but eat?

There is not much to do here, little to look forward to. Maybe that explains the craving for coffee, cigarettes, sugar. Chain smokers exhale billows and clouds, fingers brown, breath rank. Cotton-mouthed from medication, we amble to the water fountain but prefer something caffeinated, preferably Coke. Standard-issue coffee is weak swill, but it's guzzled in abundance. Vending machines dispense instant coffee, sodas, cookies, and chips, which we purchase with coins from our allowances, if we can find a staff member to accompany us.

Beneath the constant restlessness on the ward there is a suspension of anticipation; we are caught in the sludge of the slow-moving present. Something is missing—that force that keeps a bicycle balanced when your feet aren't touching the ground. That leap of faith that enables people to go forward, to do, is tenuous here, fragile. The innate belief in forward motion has been damaged, replaced with belief in other realities: pain, dark forces, the power of gravity . . . which pulls people from their chairs to the floor, from tops of buildings to sidewalks.

I am on constant observation. I sit outside the nurse's station, where they can watch me. A girl sits down next to me. Shiny brown hair, pretty heart-shaped face. She seems to be my age, but more developed, possessing a curvy feminine body. We introduce ourselves. Her name is Margaret but she calls herself Marjee.

"How old are you?" I ask.

"Thirteen," she answers. She tells me she is from Oklahoma, recently come to live in New York with her mother. She is here because of a quasi-suicide attempt. "It was only twenty aspirin, but they pumped my stomach anyway," she says, smiling a beautiful smile. Looking into her long-lashed brown eyes, I recognize a friend. Marjee likes to draw and paint and read; she also cooks, sews, sings, and tells long stories with imaginative, humorous plots. She doesn't think of herself as a writer, but I am in awe.

Marjee and I graduate from observation at the same time. When we move from small observation A-dorm to the larger B-dorm, we choose adjacent beds. I introduce her to Camus; she sews me a pair of elephant bellbottoms. I give her one of my Rapidograph pens; together we make funny drawings. We read poems aloud, whisper late at night, weep and comfort each other, write notes and giggle. "Sweet dreams," we wish each other before sleep.

I get to know the other adolescents. Laurie, tough, street-smart girl from Long Island, carefully applies full makeup each morning, shaving off her eyebrows and penciling them back on. She's had an abortion, taken hard drugs. Harold, sweet bad boy with a Dutch boy haircut, lifts weights, gets into playful boxing matches with staff and patients. Nick, resident sadist, with his handsome WASP looks, has plenty of budding young female masochists to play with. Scornful, sexy, and acerbic, he enjoys administering Indian burns on arms and legs, and other chosen punishments, physical and psychological, upon a group of willing slaves who do his ironing, shine his shoes in exchange for sexual attention. Rocky is Nick's best friend; skinny, graceful, smart, with her rueful sense of humor and steady blue-gray gaze, shiny hip-length hair swinging like a whip around a weed. Rocky spends too much time in the shower, washing and scrubbing until her skin is bright red. What is she scrubbing away? We never find out, because in spite of therapy, denial seems to be the rule of thumb. Like shut mollusks, we sit tight in our undersea world, waiting it out on the ocean floor.

The adolescents attend school three hours a day, in classrooms on the fourth and fifth floors where we study literature, math, and history. Our English teacher, Mrs. Gould, with her jangling Moroccan bangles, huge earrings, African pendants, brightly woven textiles, and Jewish Afro, loves us dearly, and tells us so. "My brilliant children!" she calls us. She teaches Shakespeare, Blake, Lawrence, Eliot, Yeats, Lorca, Dostoyevsky, Tolstoy, and we love her back. It is impossible not to. She is always on our side, dismayed when clothing gives way to pajamas, or when one of us appears in class red-eyed and out of it.

On the ward, we listen to music. It's the 1960s, the age of Aquarius. The Beatles release *Sgt. Pepper,* followed by *The White Album.* Mick Jagger wails "Gimme Shelter"; Janis Joplin screams the blues. Eric Clapton coaxes voices from the strings of his guitar. Leonard Cohen moans "Suzanne"; The Velvet Underground groans "Heroin." The boys blast Led Zeppelin on the stereo until a nurse comes and turns the volume down. Harold struts like a rooster, singing, "I can't get no . . . sat-is-fac-shun." We hear about Woodstock; I am miserable to have missed it. Then we hear about Altamont and I don't feel so bad. Jim Morrison, bard of darkness, kills his father and rapes his mother in a song; courting his death, he is one of our own kind.

We watch television. On the news we witness the slow de-escalation of the war and the latest student protests. Our favorite programs are *Mission Impossible, Secret Agent, The Fugitive, The Prisoner—* all about people trying to escape tight situations. Sometimes there's a movie, which we watch with lights out, taking us through the evening. There's a strict 11 p.m. curfew. If the movie runs long, we're out of luck. The night of the moonwalk broadcast, the attendant snaps the TV off right before the famous line, "One small step for man, one giant leap for mankind."

The adolescents line up for fainting sessions, administered by Nick. He puts his hands around the neck of each willing victim and squeezes until he or she faints. I'm amazed to feel my senses go thin, dissolving into a rush of darkness, my body melting away. I barely feel Nick lowering me to the living room floor. It is almost as good as drugs.

We pay an attendant to get us drugs, which we share with him, four or five of us sitting in a private room smoking grass or hash, trying not to splutter loudly when we exhale, laughing as we get higher and higher. Then we become desperately paranoid, certain at every sound that we are busted. The next day we avoid this same attendant, who is suddenly cool and formal.

Marjee and I get high on Romilar with codeine, chug a fifth of gin, get so sick that to this day I retch at the smell of gin. The world twirls. We throw up all afternoon and night, waking the next morning bone dry and empty. Dizzy and weak, we are in a ton of trouble.

"Inappropriate behavior!" the doctors tell us. *Appropriate* and *inappropriate* are the standards by which we live, by which privileges are meted out or taken away. "Inappropriate acting out! No phone privileges, no clothing privileges, no outside passes."

It is also inappropriate to ask too many questions, to swear, to get angry, to laugh too loudly, to have physical contact. "Inappropriate acting out," my sexuality; my crushes on boys quickly boiling down to sexual escapades. "Inappropriate physical contact," they write in my chart. I am put back on observation. "Not allowed off the ward except for school." No more trips to the vending machines, to the gym, the caged-in roof.

What is appropriate behavior? I ask. Particularly for adolescents, with our twitchy energy, uncommunicative moodiness, rising sexuality, innate rebelliousness, and contrary insistence on questioning authority. Where are we to funnel our energy, intelligence, mischief, pain, and rage? Is it inappropriate to want to go outside, walk in the daylight, breathe fresh air, be among the living, pick the grass, see the sky, streets? Not to mention explore new interests, be alone on occasion, have some privacy? And what of our need to connect?

I fight back, continue to do what people my age do. I have crushes; I fall in love: with James, the sad violinist, tender and pale, wet-lipped and moist-palmed when we kiss. But first, and mostly, with Nick, our resident sexy sadist. We bribe a night guard to leave us alone together. I lose my virginity straddling Nick in an armchair in the living room, after hours.

"No PC!" is the rule on the ward. Patients are not allowed to touch one another, certainly not sexually. But there are ways around this. I have PC—physical contact—with an assortment of male patients, in chairs, corners, the phone booth, wedged behind doors. I am caught doing inappropriate things in tight places. Hopeless about deterring me, my doctor prescribes birth control pills, which, in addition to the Thorazine, encourages my body to bloat and swell. Will they ever guess that in touching each other, we are trying to make contact, to connect?

Christmas holidays approach, a turbulent parting of the waters. Some patients get passes to go home to their families; among those left on the ward, spirits are low. It is too quiet; the minutes drag. Acts of kindness on the part of the staff help get us through the days. We are surprised on Christmas day by presents for each of us; a group of staff members has chipped in to buy us gifts, specially chosen for each person. I get a pair of glass bead earrings, blue and green, bringing out the green in my hazel eyes. The mood on the ward lightens. We toast each other with alcohol-free eggnog, eat turkey and stuffing, sing carols, and go to bed peacefully.

A week or so later, several of the staff members who gave us gifts are fired; others are transferred to different wards or forced to work the late night shift. They have broken a cardinal rule—no giving of gifts to patients by staff. But this was so personal, so human, and so needed, we protest, not a trace of wrongdoing or coercion, just kindness. Like children, we are told these rules are for our own good. We go on sit-down strike, to no avail. "Inappropriate behavior," the catch-22 of life inside, has now backlashed against those of our keepers who were caring enough to show it. We feel a new bond. Over time, a few staff members return, and our protest settles into resignation.

On occasion we are herded into the boxy elevator and transported to a rooftop on the eleventh floor where the building narrows, forming a stepped-back tier, caged by a chain-link fence. The nurse unlocks the door and I am hit in the face with a blast of light and richly fragrant air. Below us, the Hudson stretches, a shimmering band. The sight is dizzying. I refocus my eyes on the fence that holds us in, holds us back, then drop my gaze to the concrete floor. I join the others; we pace, walking round and round, back and forth.

One day on the roof I meet a girl a few years older than me. An unfortunate girl, I can see—bad skin, thin hair, face a mask of pain. She picks her lips and skin, scratches her arms. The others avoid her. Yet when I smile, she smiles back, transformed.

"Hi," she says softly, her pale blue eyes looking up at me.

Her name is Helen. I ask her how long she's been here. She tells me a year and a half. An infinity of time. . . . Though my heart moves toward her in sympathy, I take a step back in fear. I wonder, will I be like her in a year?

As we talk Helen shifts her weight from one foot to the other, rocking side to side, and before I know it she is clutching at her arms, her voice rising in tremulous questions, crying in little bleats. "Do you think there's hope for us? Do you think we'll ever get out of here? Will you be my friend?"

I take the ring off my finger and give it to Helen. The ring, a black stone in a silver setting, was a birthday present from my best friend. Regret vies with the compassion and empathy, revulsion and fear battling in my chest. Back on the ward, when I feel the empty place on my finger, I remember our conversation. *Is there hope for us? Will we ever get out of here? Will you be my friend?* I ask myself.

A few months later, Helen is given a private room on our ward. She is recovering from a broken back, in a body brace from hips to shoulders, after jumping from the roof of a neighborhood building. She keeps to herself a lot, but I often hear her crying in her little bleats, see her picking at the scabs on her arms, legs, and face.

One day she disappears. "Where is Helen? Has anyone seen her?" We hold our breath for a day, until they break the news. She has jumped again from a building, but is alive. Seemingly indestructible, she pushes the limits of survival. They've sent her to the acute ward. No visitors allowed. A week or two later the word filters down: "Have you heard about Helen?" Somehow she has gotten hold of matches and lighter fluid; set herself on fire. I shudder to think of the flames dancing over the surface of her skin, that sensitive boundary that defines the self, leaving it raw and scarred. I know she won't be coming back downstairs for a long, long time.

Then I get the word: they are shipping her. "Shipping" is the hospital jargon used when a patient is sent to a regular state hospital. Creedmore, Rockland, Manhattan State—those fearsome institutions that warehouse chronic cases. "If you act out again, we might have to ship you," is the ultimate threat. *Shipped,* the word spoken in a fearful whisper—like packages, cargo. Patients are shipped as punishment or if they're considered too much of a risk. Rocky is shipped to Rockland and never returns; Nick's cynicism hardens into malevolent bitterness. When Marjee is caught smoking a joint, they ship her to Rockland, fourteen years old and terrified. It's lonely on the ward without her. When Marjee returns three months later, she is brittle, fearful, despairing. I ask what it was like there. "Hell," she says, but won't discuss it.

* * *

After a long while, I can wear my own clothes. I even get to go outside. Several times a week a staff member accompanies small groups on neighborhood excursions. My first steps outside are oddly dreamlike, the sounds and smells of the street a phantom of a former life. We walk two blocks to the Shangri-La Diner, where we crowd into a booth and try not to embarrass our escort. We order coffee and sandwiches with extra pickles (anything to spice up our lives) to bring back for friends on the ward. Then we return, the bland blond building at the end of 168th Street drawing us to it like a magnet, our temporary powers of locomotion disappearing as we descend in the elevator.

It is spring. We are escorted on an outing to Riverside Park. We take the elevator down to the deserted entrance on Riverside Drive, navigate the whizzing cars, cross the parkway, and enter the park. The air is sweet with grass and pollen; sunlight sparkles on the river. We unpack picnic baskets, explore the park. Marjee and Harold disappear into some tall grass. The hot sun glares in my eyes; I feel a headache coming on. Somehow the fresh, fragrant air saddens me— though I'm out in it today, I know I am just a visitor; it is air meant for others, not me.

One day when I am trusted enough to go to the vending machines unattended, I get on the elevator, say "Ten, please," stroll past the guard in the lobby, and walk out the door. I come alive in the chilly autumn air. Before I know it I am blocks away. I have *eloped*.

"Eloping" is hospitalese for escape. Since eloping in the romantic sense generally involves another person, who exactly are we eloping with, aside from ourselves? Perhaps our freedom, our own free will. "Have you heard? So-and-so eloped!"—the news rips through the ward like a fire; when it reaches me I am alight with admiration and envy. "Good for them!" I gloat, and the desire to accomplish this on my own builds, burns.

Eloping takes some planning: eluding the staff, thinking up a good story to tell the elevator operator, finding a way to change into street clothes; finally, walking out that door. Marjee and I spend an afternoon together in Central Park. When we return we're put back on observation, but it was worth it. Eloping becomes our major pastime. We take turns helping each other escape. But it is hard to stay out there; we are teenage girls with less than average resiliency. We bounce against the limits of our independence and ricochet right back inside. Then it's back to pajamas and observation, until we slowly win back the trust of the staff.

The time has come to be assigned a new psychiatrist. The ward bubbles with excitement and apprehension. "Who'd you get?" we whisper, "Oh, he's nice," or "He's cute," like school kids talking about their new teachers. Suicide attempts crop up like weeds; it is a busy season for the quiet room. When I was assigned my last doctor, I was weak-kneed with mortification. He was too attractive; how could I talk to him? I sat, jiggling my leg, trying to come up with fitting Freudian tidbits to feed him, only hinting at what I really felt. I saw him for almost a year, twice a week for thirty minutes, simmering in embarrassment.

When I meet my new, pleasantly ordinary-looking shrink, my relief is palpable. I can tell he's shy, just as I am. He has a slight speech impediment. I talk to him a little. He listens, responds, warmly. When I say or do something outrageous he is just as embarrassed as I am, reddening and stuttering in his gentle way, lifting his shoulders in a stymied shrug.

He sits with me through my silences, enjoys my sense of irony and humor. I start to let down my guard. When I confide the painful emotions I often have listening to others, feeling that I have nothing of my own to contribute, my doctor tells me, "Being a good listener is a talent in itself." That little bit of support is a talisman I carry with me, a touchstone of self-worth. So much more than these drugs and extreme measures they treat me with, I need a friend, an adult I can trust, nonjudgmental, on my side. That, more than anything else, is what I need. But it comes too late, and too briefly.

Midyear, my doctor informs me of his decision to become a child psychologist; he's been offered a position elsewhere and has decided to accept. Even though I put up a tough exterior, I manage to tell him I am sorry he has to go, that I will miss him. I envy those children who will, early on, have the chance to experience his gentle presence.

I start experiencing new symptoms: the scene in front of me grows gauzy and dissolves; objects shimmer, threatening to vanish. I have a headache that won't go away. When I complain of these things, my medication is increased, and I feel more and more depressed.

One morning I am washing my face and become aware of a voice droning in my head. I can almost make out words, but what I really hear is its nagging, critical tone. Suddenly, I recognize the voice. It's my mother's voice in my head. I can't make it stop.

Later that day I get an idea for something new to do. I ask for my razor to shave my legs, remove the blade, and hide it in my towel. "There's no blade!" I tell the attendant. She goes to get me a new one. When she isn't looking, I put the old one back in and stash the new one carefully under my soap.

In the bathroom stall I roll up my pajama sleeve, then change my mind and unsnap the top, pulling the sleeve down to expose my shoulder and upper arm. I unwrap the blade and hold it between thumb and forefinger, enjoying the feel of its almost dimensionless thinness, the contradictory flexibility of the metal. The razor's edge—a Zen koan of a concept. A weapon against myself, but more specifically against those who have denied me my freedom. I am the samurai, empowered by my own will.

Holding the blade against the smooth surface of my upper arm, I slice quickly, then open my eyes to look at the two-inch slash, just for an instant, before the blood wells up and drips out, a crimson tear. All I feel is a slight stinging. The skin parts to reveal spongy white fat cells; I'm able to see inside myself and find flesh and blood, not just emptiness and confusion. *Alive!* I am relieved of the pressure that had built up inside me. After making a second, parallel cut, I place wads of tissue against my flesh until the bleeding subsides, pull my pajama top carefully over my arm, flush the toilet, and walk past the nurse's station, triumphantly concealing my secret. I repeat this process several times on both arms and thighs until one day a nurse notices a red line seeping through my pajama sleeve.

"I wasn't trying to kill myself," I protest when I'm put back on observation. They don't understand; I do it because the blade lends me its power.

I am tired of being here, tired of feeling sluggish and confined, tired of the daily routines, the bland food, the stale air, the buzz and whine of consciousness. I am tired of being.

I have no desire to do the busywork that Maggie, the occupational therapist, offers me. I don't want to sew, or stitch a wallet from a kit. I categorically refuse to weave a basket. I am feeling too failed and up- tight to want to draw, my former passion. When I put a pencil to pa- per, I draw a line that curls around in tight concentric spirals, until it ends, trapped within itself.

While looking through Maggie's supplies I notice a jar labeled "POISON: Contains Petroleum Distillates. DO NOT DRINK." In- trigued, I take a closer look. It is grout sealer, a silicon-based cement used in making mosaic tiles. Each time I go to OT, I court that jar, waiting for the right moment. What do I have to lose? I'm stuck here until I'm eighteen. Summer is coming and I don't want to be around to smell the air and wish I was outside.

The moment arrives when I am left alone for a few minutes while Maggie hustles a disruptive patient outside. I glide to the cabinet, take the jar from the shelf, unscrew the lid. Pungent fumes attack my nose. Though the stuff smells horrible, I bring the jar to my lips, tilt back my head, and pour the vile viscous contents down my throat. Almost immediately my ears are ringing, my head pounding. I can't contain my retching. When Maggie returns she comes over and smells my noxious silicon breath, rushes away to call the ward. They make me drink an antidote—warm, soapy water—and I vomit long and thor- oughly, saving us the effort of pumping my stomach. I want to say I wish I'd never seen the jar or chosen to go that route, but I can't. It's just another passageway marked DO NOT ENTER that I am com- pelled to take.

* * *

At some point I make up my mind that I will survive this place and move on. Maybe because my eighteenth birthday is in sight, my free- dom seems less remote. Maybe because I've seen too many people come and go, I feel the time approaching for me to take my place out- side. I keep a low profile, go to school and activities, take my meds. The higher powers lower my dosage, give me neighborhood privi- leges, and offer me a volunteer job within the hospital complex. I agree to a job accompanying schoolchildren on tours of a medical research facility. I am anxious to rise to this new challenge, but also fearful. What if I'm too shy to relate to the children? What if, more confident than I am, they sense something's wrong with me?

After an initial interview, I'm shown around the facility. A young man in a white coat accompanies me to the lab. There, in cages that line the walls of the room, are the expected mice and rats, but then I see cages of cats, piled one on another, floor to ceiling. And these are not normal cats; they are cats missing the tops of their heads, on top of which have been affixed some kind of machines. The cats are meowing, and their eyes don't look right; some crouch open-mouthed, drooling; some lay motionless. A panicked horror passes through me. *A cat with a machine on its head?* This is not what a cat is supposed to look like, or be. An alien thing confined in a cage. A staring cat seems to catch me in its blank gaze, drool dripping from its open mouth. I know that look. I've seen it often on the ward.

But I am determined. The following Tuesday morning I leave the ward to meet my first batch of kids. They cluster around me endearingly with their braids, braces, questions, and lunch boxes. After lunch we are to witness a dissection. The technician wheels in a cart with a large something laying on top, covered by a sheet. A strong chemical smell fills the room. He pulls back the sheet to reveal a large black dog, lying on his side. He is too still; I want to see him wriggle onto his belly, get up, run around. The technician points out the location of the organs, tracing a line on the dog's belly with his finger, then picks up a scalpel and begins to cut. It is too much for me; the dog, the smell, the stillness. A wave of nausea takes me. "Excuse me," I mumble, and run from the room.

I never go back. "That's fine," staff says, but to me it was a cruel exercise. How could they have sent me there, where, thin-skinned as I am, I was sure to fail? I'm sad I won't see the children again. And the image of that motionless dog haunts me, reminding me of the senselessness of death, something I experience all too often in my life inside.

"Did you hear about Rocky?" We are in Mrs. Gould's classroom. The phrasing of the question contains within itself an answer; it ricochets impossibly around the room and settles inside each of us. We learn that Rocky has hung herself on a ward in Rockland State; it is horrible to imagine her life-filled body a dead weight. Nobody can offer any insight. We hug each other, weeping. Mrs. Gould takes a handkerchief from her pocket and blows her nose. She hands out tissues, little white flags of loss that become transparent with tears. One by one we remember Rocky aloud, reciting all we loved. We band together like the remaining survivors of a forgotten regiment.

There are many casualties in this war. Liz survives wrist-slicing and an attempt at suffocating herself in the laundry room with the gas-fueled clothes dryer. Over time she makes progress, spends less time on the ward, and is finally discharged. We are happy for her, until the question hits home: "Have you heard about Liz?" Without warning, she drove to her family's cabin in the woods, held her father's shotgun to her head, and in an instant blew away the thing that troubled her most, her mind.

These are my family members; it hurts to lose them. Sometimes it is so painful I want to follow them, but I have come to recognize that I will not ferry myself across that river. I have decided to stay on this side, where the living dwell.

* * *

My eighteenth birthday approaches. I sit on the card table in front of the staircase door swinging my legs. "Get off of that table," I am told. "Why?" I ask, "I'm just sitting here." I anticipate the nurse's answer before it comes. "Because it's inappropriate. Go sit in a chair." I ignore her and swing my legs a little faster. The nurse calls the male attendant and they both approach me. "If you don't get off that table now, you will be taken off." I do not move. The nurse nods to the attendant, a large powerful man, who walks toward me. I jump off the table, but it is too late. He tackles me with his full weight, and I am dragged down the hall to the quiet room, shot full of sodium amytal, tied into a straitjacket, and locked in. Twenty-four hours later I am sent to another floor, my belongings dumped into a laundry bag; within days I am shipped to Manhattan State Hospital. This is the final insult—without being allowed to say goodbye to my friends, I am manhandled, drugged, and locked up . . . for sitting on a table. It is as if the hospital has to have the last word; unsuccessful in "treating" me, they can at least show me who's boss.

It could have been worse. In the old days of asylums, I could have been tortured, tube-fed, given electric shock, even surgically subdued. Being sent to Manhattan State reminds me just how fortunate I've been.

Manhattan State Hospital is a warehouse for lost souls, located on an island in the middle of the East River. From the Queens side of the Triborough bridge approach ramp, you can see the sun shining clear through the windows, not a moving body in sight.

The ward stinks of urine and unwashed flesh. All night I lie awake on a cot listening to the snores, snorts, sighs, whistling breath, and night terrors of the thirty women I share the dorm with. The staff are uncompromising—I witness an attendant cruelly shove an elderly woman against a wall for not wanting to wait in line for her medication. Tasteless meals are eaten in complete silence. Toilets have no seats or stalls; shit is smeared on the walls.

One day I see a ghost in the dining room. It is Helen. She shuffles along with terrified eyes. I see the tough pink scars from the fire on her neck and hands. I try to talk to her, but an attendant stops me. After breakfast I greet her in the hallway; she takes both my hands and cries without sound, happy to see me. Helen spends most of her days locked in seclusion. I find ways to talk to her, whispering through the keyhole. I am fearful for her ever getting out of this place; I tell her over and over that she *will* get better, she *will* get out. Whenever I can I hug her. I pray day and night—for Helen, as well as all these women who have lived here for months or years, and for myself, young and healthy enough to walk out of here and never be locked up again. Within a month I am free.

* * *

It is scarcely a month since my release from Manhattan State. I am back in my old bedroom in my mother's apartment. I feel like a war veteran, wounded and shell-shocked, out of place in my brightly oblivious surrounds.

The phone rings. It's Harold. We chat for a minute or two.

"Have you heard about Marjee?" The question knocks the breath out of me; my mind reels as I stretch to fathom the abyss of nonbeing. From my throat comes a wail of mourning.

"She overdosed," says Harold. During those first months after Marjee escaped, she had begun using heroin—shooting sleep deeply into the hidden source of her pain; dissolving herself into the oblivion she longed for. Or did she? We'll never know whether Marjee intended to kill herself, or if it was an accidental overdose.

The thing is, I helped her escape. I will go on to live my life, but Marjee will never reach her eighteenth birthday.

I have scars, and I have dreams. I dream that Marjee and I meet as adults. "You're alive!" I cry, overcome with joy. I dream that I am back in the hospital, trying to convince them to let me out, that I have a job and clients, work to do, rent to pay, plants to water, a life to live. *Just wait,* they say, *and take your medication. Maybe in two, three months. . . .* I try to persuade them to let me use the phone, but they won't allow it. Then I wake up.

I always wear T-shirts with short sleeves to cover my scars, never tank tops. I am ashamed of my former battle scars, now an inscription of my past, marking me as different. I cringe when anyone uses the word "crazy," particularly in relation to me, or other women. I know something they do not—that so-called sanity and craziness is a continuum of many shades of gray, labeled to protect people from their fears of losing control. Doctors prescribe drugs that deaden, distancing people from their emotions, making them strangers to themselves. It is important to learn management skills, but I believe that people have souls, not just chemistry.

Later, I move into my own apartment, work part-time, take college classes. I join a grassroots political action group, Mental Patients Liberation Project (MPLP), working to change legislation so that mental patients can no longer be held in institutions against their will. We travel to hospitals, staying overnight on locked wards in order to inform patients of their rights and give them some hope about life outside.

I struggle with my sense of belonging in the world. Will I ever simply feel a part of life, not undermined by a sense of lost time and lost innocence? It takes years to learn how to befriend myself, live healthily, have relationships, find meaningful work, develop my skills as an artist. After a long while I give up cigarettes. I never take drugs. I allow myself alcohol and coffee, but that's all. I struggle drugless through depressions. I stay away from psychiatrists. There is help along the way: the Tibetan Buddhist Jungian psychologist who sees me free of charge for several years and urges me to develop compassion toward myself. People who encourage and support my artistic efforts, and wonderful friends. Life supports me, and I float, even learn to swim. I cultivate my freedom, finding it hard to be confined in any way. Over time my scars fade to the faintest of marks. My life takes on a more regular shape. I am rarely visited by panic or fall into bottomless pits. I am just like everyone else, almost.

*   *   *

1987. Saturday afternoon, late fall. I lie in bed reading, savoring a day off from my job as a magazine designer. The phone rings.

"Is this Mindy Lewis?" I confirm, ask who's calling.

"This is Dr. N from the N.Y.S. Psychiatric Institute." Something quakes within my chest. He explains that he is conducting a series of twenty-year follow-up interviews. He wants to ask me some questions; would I consider setting up an interview?

My throat closes up; I am having a panic reaction. Why should I be afraid? He can't lock me up just for talking to him. Then I notice another emotion: vivid, passionate anger.

I decide to do it. I have a lot to say to this man. We set up a time for a phone interview. By the time the phone rings, I am ready. We go over basic information, filling in each other's blanks. He pumps me for details about my friends: Marjee, Rocky, Liz, Nick. I tell him about meeting with Nick after P.I.—how he seemed to decline, malevolence eating away his charm and good looks. The last time I saw him, his tongue flicked lizard-like in and out of his mouth in an indescribably evil manner (I later discover this is a common side effect of long-term use of antidepressants). When someone finally asked, "Did you hear about Nick?" I was not surprised.

And Marjee. What depth of unhappiness drove her to destroy herself? I recall Marjee's stories about her flighty mother, stern grandmother, and alcoholic father, who used to beat her with his belt. I search my hazy memory for clues of sexual abuse, but if it existed, it remains locked in the past.

Dr. N is particularly interested in incest. "Nobody asked about it back then," he says. But subtle clues had fluttered everywhere, like butterflies caught in our hair, wings moving the air. This one's love of her brother, hate of her uncle, fear of her father; Rocky's endless scrubbing.

I ask about Helen; to my great relief I am told she's alive and well somewhere on the West Coast.

Dr. N asks how my life has been since the hospital. I recap my significant events: my work with MPLP, excelling at college but never graduating, having long relationships but not marrying, living in my apartment all these years. I tell him I am fine; I work, I paint, I don't take drugs or see a shrink, I am completely fine! In spite of the hospital, I add.

"Is there anything else you'd like to tell me?" I wind up and let him have it: about being confined, misdiagnosed, medicated, traumatized; a shy, frightened, arrogant adolescent who takes years to live down an early, unnecessary, too-long incarceration in a loony bin. How hard it's been.

"I'm sorry," he says. "We didn't know very much about treating adolescents in those days." And that is it. Two hours on the phone, and I have reached back twenty years into the past and spoken for that girl who couldn't speak for herself, and receive an answer and an apology—skimpy and scant and too late to make any real difference. And finally, I face that girl and claim her, embrace her and love her, knowing that she is an important part of me, that we are one.

Ode to Carrie White

Elayne Clift

Who were you, Carrie White,
that you had the stamina
to stay in this world
for 116 years?

What did you do that night,
that so scared your husband,
John, that he locked you up
for 81 years?

Why did you yield without
a fight, and begin
to believe "crazy"
after 35 years?

When did you first lose sight
of your power, your will,
your life force? After
how many years, Carrie White?

And where is your sweet soul now?

*(Carrie White died in 1991, after being incarcerated in a Florida mental
hospital since 1909)*

From *The Bell Jar*

Sylvia Plath

I woke warm and placid in my white cocoon. A shaft of pale, wintry sunlight dazzled the mirror and the glasses on the bureau and the metal doorknobs. From across the hall came the early-morning clatter of the maids in the kitchen, preparing the breakfast trays.

I heard the nurse knock on the door next to mine, at the far end of the hall. Mrs. Savage's sleepy voice boomed out, and the nurse went in to her with the jingling tray. I thought, with a mild stir of pleasure, of the steaming blue china coffee pitcher and the blue china breakfast cup and the fat blue china cream jug with the white daisies on it.

I was beginning to resign myself.

If I was going to fall, I would hang on to my small comforts, at least, as long as I possibly could.

The nurse rapped on my door and, without waiting for an answer, breezed in.

It was a new nurse—they were always changing—with a lean, sand-colored face and sandy hair, and large freckles polka-dotting her bony nose. For some reason the sight of this nurse made me sick at heart, and it was only as she strode across the room to snap up the green blind that I realized part of her strangeness came from being empty-handed.

I opened my mouth to ask for my breakfast tray, but silenced myself immediately. The nurse would be mistaking me for somebody else. New nurses often did that. Somebody in Belsize must be having shock treatments, unknown to me, and the nurse had, quite understandably, confused me with her.

I waited until the nurse had made her little circuit of my room, patting, straightening, arranging, and taken the next tray in to Loubelle one door farther down the hall.

Then I shoved my feet into my slippers, dragging my blanket with me, for the morning was bright, but very cold, and crossed quickly to the kitchen. The pink-uniformed maid was filling a row of blue china coffee pitchers from a great, battered kettle on the stove.

I looked with love at the lineup of waiting trays—the white paper napkins, folded in their crisp, isosceles triangles, each under the anchor of its silver fork, the pale domes of soft-boiled eggs in the blue egg cups, the scalloped glass shells of orange marmalade. All I had to do was reach out and claim my tray, and the world would be perfectly normal.

"There's been a mistake," I told the maid, leaning over the counter and speaking in a low, confidential tone. "The new nurse forgot to bring in my breakfast tray today."

I managed a bright smile, to show there were no hard feelings.

"What's the name?"

"Greenwood. Esther Greenwood."

"Greenwood, Greenwood, Greenwood." The maid's warty index finger slid down the list of names of the patients in Belsize tacked up on the kitchen wall. "Greenwood, no breakfast today."

I caught the rim of the counter with both hands.

"There must be a mistake. Are you sure it's Greenwood?"

"Greenwood," the maid said decisively as the nurse came in.

The nurse looked questioningly from me to the maid.

"Miss Greenwood wanted her tray," the maid said, avoiding my eyes.

"Oh," the nurse smiled at me, "you'll be getting your tray later on this morning, Miss Greenwood. You . . ."

But I didn't wait to hear what the nurse said. I strode blindly out into the hall, not to my room, because that was where they would come to get me, but to the alcove, greatly inferior to the alcove at Caplan, but an alcove, nevertheless, in a quiet corner of the hall, where John and Loubelle and DeeDee and Mrs. Savage would not come.

I curled up in the far corner of the alcove with the blanket over my head. It wasn't the shock treatment that struck me, so much as the bare-faced treachery of Doctor Nolan. I liked Doctor Nolan, I loved her, I had given her my trust on a platter and told her everything, and she had promised, faithfully, to warn me ahead of time if ever I had to have another shock treatment.

If she had told me the night before I would have lain awake all night, of course, full of dread and foreboding, but by morning I would have been composed and ready. I would have gone down the hall between two nurses, past DeeDee and Loubelle and Mrs. Savage and Joan, with dignity, like a person coolly resigned to execution.

The nurse bent over me and called my name.

I pulled away and crouched farther into the corner. The nurse disappeared. I knew she would return, in a minute, with two burly men attendants, and they would bear me, howling and hitting, past the smiling audience now gathered in the lounge.

Doctor Nolan put her arm around me and hugged me like a mother.

"You said you'd *tell* me!" I shouted at her through the dishevelled blanket.

"But I *am* telling you," Doctor Nolan said. "I've come specially early to tell you, and I'm taking you over myself."

I peered at her through swollen lids. "Why didn't you tell me last night?"

"I only thought it would keep you awake. If I'd known . . ."

"You *said* you'd tell me."

"Listen, Esther," Doctor Nolan said. "I'm going over with you. I'll be there the whole time, so everything will happen right, the way I promised. I'll be there when you wake up, and I'll bring you back again."

I looked at her. She seemed very upset.

I waited a minute. Then I said, "Promise you'll be there."

"I promise."

Doctor Nolan took out a white handkerchief and wiped my face. Then she hooked her arm in my arm, like an old friend, and helped me up, and we started down the hall. My blanket tangled about my feet, so I let it drop, but Doctor Nolan didn't seem to notice. We passed Joan, coming out of her room, and I gave her a meaning, disdainful smile, and she ducked back and waited until we had gone by.

Then Doctor Nolan unlocked a door at the end of the hall and led me down a flight of stairs into the mysterious basement corridors that linked, in an elaborate network of tunnels and burrows, all the various buildings of the hospital.

The walls were bright, white lavatory tile with bald bulbs set at intervals in the black ceiling. Stretchers and wheelchairs were beached here and there against the hissing, knocking pipes that ran and branched in an intricate nervous system along the glittering walls. I hung on to Doctor Nolan's arm like death, and every so often she gave me an encouraging squeeze.

Finally, we stopped at a green door with Electrotherapy printed on it in black letters. I held back, and Doctor Nolan waited. Then I said, "Let's get it over with," and we went in.

The only people in the waiting room besides Doctor Nolan and me were a pallid man in a shabby maroon bathrobe and his accompanying nurse.

"Do you want to sit down?" Doctor Nolan pointed at a wooden bench, but my legs felt full of heaviness, and I thought how hard it would be to hoist myself from a sitting position when the shock treatment people came in.

"I'd rather stand."

At last a tall, cadaverous woman in a white smock entered the room from an inner door. I thought that she would go up and take the man in the maroon bathrobe, as he was first, so I was surprised when she came toward me.

"Good morning, Doctor Nolan," the woman said, putting her arm around my shoulders. "Is this Esther?"

"Yes, Miss Huey. Esther, this is Miss Huey, she'll take good care of you. I've told her about you."

I thought the woman must be seven feet tall. She bent over me in a kind way, and I could see that her face, with the buck teeth protruding in the center, had at one time been badly pitted with acne. It looked like maps of the craters on the moon.

"I think we can take you right away, Esther," Miss Huey said. "Mr. Anderson won't mind waiting, will you, Mr. Anderson?"

Mr. Anderson didn't say a word, so with Miss Huey's arm around my shoulder, and Doctor Nolan following, I moved into the next room.

Through the slits of my eyes, which I didn't dare open too far, lest the full view strike me dead, I saw the high bed with its white, drumtight sheet, and the machine behind the bed, and the masked person—I couldn't tell whether it was a man or a woman—behind the machine, and other masked people flanking the bed on both sides.

Miss Huey helped me climb up and lie down on my back.

"Talk to me," I said.

Miss Huey began to talk in a low, soothing voice, smoothing the salve on my temples and fitting the small electric buttons on either side of my head. "You'll be perfectly all right, you won't feel a thing, just bite down. . . ." And she set something on my tongue and in panic I bit down, and darkness wiped me out like chalk on a blackboard.

For Love Nor Money

Anonymous

From the moment I awoke, I began battling urges to swallow entire bottles of pills. By 11:00 a.m. I had the pills spread out before me. I called my therapist and left her a message: *I am feeling suicidal. I have all my pills in front of me and I feel out of control.*

It took me a while to work up to those words. I spent the first five minutes of the message talking about bad dreams I'd had. Bob Dylan blared in the background. My therapist, a psychologist I had been working with for six years, didn't understand the urgency of the situation. My suicidality was nothing new to her, nor were my long ramblings on her message machine. I had asked her to call me back, and she did—three hours later. By that time, I was already on my way to the hospital, where my true nightmare really started.

For three hours, as I waited for my therapist to call, I read T. S. Eliot. I wrote about my feelings. I slashed pieces of paper with a pen. I drew cuts on my wrist in red ink. And, in stages, I prepared my poison. First, I crushed all my antidepressants with a hammer, catching the orange powder on a paper towel. This was a pivotal step: once I had crushed them, a confrontation would be necessary; for if I were going to continue taking them, I would have to get a new prescription from my psychiatrist, Dr. F. She would ask me what happened to the drugs I had. I would have to tell her I had hammered them up. She would ask why. We would have a discussion.

And a discussion was necessary. I was in a creative writing program, working on a poetry thesis, and the drugs were blunting my feelings. When I sat down to write, I felt nothing inside me. Dr. F. had suggested changing to another drug or adding a tiny amount of lithium to the current one, but either experiment terrified me. I did not want to become even more unrecognizable to myself.

I had started antidepressants nearly a year before, when after several episodes of severe, suicidal depression, my psychologist had given me an ultimatum: either you take antidepressants, or I stop working with you. I couldn't stand the thought of starting over with another therapist, so I had agreed. At first, the drugs worked. I was happy for the first time in decades. For the first time in my life, I wrote poetry about joy. As the months passed, however, the drugs did less to quell the depression. When we increased the dosage, I started to feel out of control of my poetry, my body, and my life. My therapist seemed to understand, but she was adamant about her requirements for working with me.

Each morning I had to face the decision: Do I take a pill and allow myself to be controlled by the drugs, or do I resist? This was one morning too many.

To the orange powder I added ten Percocet, stirring the mixture into a glass of orange juice. That's when I called my psychiatrist's emergency number. After forty-five minutes, my patience thinned. I felt abandoned.

As I watched starlings wheeling across the November sky, I thought, this could be my last view of life. And I began to drink.

I didn't really want to die. I wanted to make a gesture, to express my rage at life. I wanted to stop thinking, to stop feeling, to sleep if I could. And I wanted to exit the trap of choosing between my therapist and antidepressants. I felt I couldn't quit therapy, and I couldn't continue taking the drugs. I was hoping that with this gesture I could shift one of the factors in the equation or at least have the satisfaction of rebellion.

Before I drank anymore, I tried my psychiatrist again. As the minutes passed with no return call, I took several more gulps of the mixture.

Even as I drank, I knew it was a bad idea. Finally, I called a hotline. After several tries, I got through and spoke to a young man who kept me talking while he checked the dose I had taken and calibrated its effects, given my height and weight.

"That combination is lethal," he finally said. "To be frank with you, I'm scared. If we send a taxi, will you go to the hospital?"

At that moment, my psychiatrist came through on call waiting. I explained the situation, and she said to go to the nearest emergency room.

"But what will I tell them?" I asked her.

"Exactly what you told me. The truth."

I'm on a long white table, surrounded by people. A white-haired doctor with a foreign accent brushes back the curtains. "Why you do this?" he demands.

Flat on my back, sleepy from drugs, and surrounded by strangers, I am in no position to answer a syntactically challenged physician. The only reply I have is a lie: "I don't know."

The doctor talks about pumping my stomach.

"Is that really necessary?" I explain that I drank only half the mixture, and most of the medicine was at the bottom of the glass.

"Yes, it's necessary. You took enough to kill a horse!"

He leaves me alone with a young nurse, who runs through my options: a tube through my nose or down my throat. I choose the throat.

"It may hurt a little," she says. She seems to be concerned about me, someone I can confide in. I turn my head to her.

"I really tried hard not to do it."

I work at being calm as the tube is passed down my throat and the contents of my stomach are expressed. As I am being pumped full of charcoal, the foreign doctor appears. His manner is less brusque now. He tells me that Percocet can cause the heart to stop, so they want to keep me under observation overnight. He has called Dr. F., as I'd asked, to report on my status. He says she asked him to thank me for coming to the emergency room.

I'm feeling pretty calm now. This is all going to turn out all right.

The doctor who seems to be second-in-command, a pretty blond woman whom I like immediately, is about my age, in her early thirties. She gently asks me a few questions about my motives for taking the pills and I tell her about the antidepressant issues (and the man who just dumped me). It's almost like girl talk, and when I pull my jar of lip gloss out of my purse, I offer her some.

Of course, she recoils. "I have my own," she says, turning her head away.

But I am sleepy and full of goodwill. When two new nurses come in to catalog the contents of my purse and put my valuables and clothes away for safekeeping so that nothing can be stolen, I am grateful. I go through my purse with the nurses, handing over item after item. I hear my own voice soft and thick with the Southern accent

I'd squelched for years. "Oh, and I have sixty dollars in my coat pocket."

The nurses return for the cash and disappear with my clothes and my valuables.

My head feels heavy. I am drifting toward sleep when a large, perfumed woman bustles into the room and takes a chair near my feet.

"I'm a social worker," she announces in a loud voice. "We'll need to have a psychiatrist evaluate you, to determine whether you need to stay beyond tonight. But it won't hurt for us to get started."

Stay? I lift my head to see her dark hair, her eyelids, blue with makeup, and the name on her badge: Judy Goodfriend.

I've entered a Kafka novel.

"I put myself in a taxi and brought myself to the emergency room. If I'd been suicidal I wouldn't have done that. So why would I have to stay?"

"You overdosed, and an overdose is considered a serious suicide attempt."

"But I hardly took anything. Most of the medicine was at the bottom of the glass!" She has no answer for that other than the one she has already given, and she proceeds to bark questions at me. Some of them she answers herself. "Are you moody, irritable?"

"Not really," I mumble.

"Yes," she overrides me.

The interview lasts an hour. Then, Judy asks if I have insurance. I tell her I do but I'm paying for the hospital visit myself. I've read too much about how information on one's insurance record can be accessed by people who have no business knowing it.

Suddenly, her tone becomes menacing. "If you can't guarantee payment and we determine that you need to be hospitalized, we can't treat you here. We'll have to send you elsewhere."

"I can guarantee payment."

"Can you get a statement from your bank that you have sufficient funds?" She is standing up now.

"Yes, I can."

I'm independently wealthy, but I don't think Judy needs to know this. She would resent me if she believed me, and if she didn't believe me, she'd think I was delusional or a compulsive liar and add that to my chart. I've always paid for my therapy myself, and it would be a shame to relinquish my privacy now, when I've spent years and thousands of dollars already to protect it.

"Even if you got a statement from your bank and could produce it right now," Judy says, after a hard stare, "it's our policy to send people who aren't paying with insurance to St. Elizabeth's."

It sounds like a good Catholic hospital to me, but I can tell from the triumphant gleam in her eyes that it's supposed to be a threat.

"What's St. Elizabeth's?"

"It's a mental institution!"

"Can you send me somewhere that isn't a mental institution?" I ask, as sweetly as possible.

"I don't know. We'll see." With that she leaves.

Once alone again, I am weak with anxiety and dread. Feeling out of control of my life had prompted the overdose. I had gone to the hospital and told the truth, as Dr. F. had suggested. And now I *am* out of control of my life.

Judy returns a few minutes later with the blond doctor. "It's our policy to pay for people who are lower class and don't have insurance," the doctor says, "but we've decided that you're middle class."

I smile. I am going to correct her, but she continues.

"And I think it's best that you be honest and report this to your insurance."

"I've already phoned the psychiatrist on call," Judy puts in, placing her hands on her broad hips. "He won't evaluate you unless you're paying with insurance. That means we can't release you. And it's not our policy to keep you here." Again, she invokes St. Elizabeth's. "I'm calling your psychiatrist," Judy says finally, in response to my silence.

I give Judy her number willingly. Dr. F. is combative, brilliant, and feisty. I know she'll stand up for me.

When Judy comes back, she leans over my bed, her face stretched in a tight smile. Her voice is sticky-sweet and tense at the same time. "We'll do everything we can to keep you from going to St. E's."

The blond doctor enters the room later, with a bright face and a light step. "Guess what? We got the results of your blood test back, and the level of drugs in your blood was very low. So maybe you do want to stay here after all."

"Do I have a choice?"

"No, *here*, I mean." She motions vaguely toward the ground. "On earth."

"Oh, yes. I do."

"Anyway, the good news is, you're out of danger. You can go home!"

My cat, my apartment, my life have never seemed so sweet to me. I sit up, still a bit groggy, but eager to get back into my sweats and back into a taxi. The minutes pass, though, and no one brings me my clothes or my purse.

I become aware of whispering outside my door.

Finally the blond doctor enters, her face tense and expressionless. "We can't let you go until you've been evaluated by a psychiatrist. We've called everyone on our list, and we can't find anyone who's willing to come if you're not paying with insurance. So you'll have to stay here overnight. I'm sure we can get a psychiatrist for you tomorrow morning."

People I haven't seen before wheel me up to the second floor. A nurse begins moistening the suction cups of an EKG, then attaches it to my chest.

"If you try to take this off," the nurse says, putting the last cup in place, "it will set off an alarm at the front desk. Also, you'll have a sitter with you all night."

A sitter. How humiliating.

The room is bleak. There is no furniture, other than a hard wooden chair in the corner, and the shower in the bathroom lacks a curtain. The nurse makes a remark about a long stay for me.

I have to talk to my therapist. I leave a message on her machine, telling her she must call me before 10:00 p.m. because after that I am not allowed to receive calls. I watch the clock. The sitter comes in as the nurse leaves. She is a young black woman whose accent is African or Caribbean. She pulls her head scarf more tightly over her hair and places herself in the corner, by my head. I listen to the EKG scrawl out the rhythms of my heart, knowing everyone knows my heart is fine, that I could even have been released.

At quarter to ten, my therapist calls back. I remember speaking through sobs. "I'm here for the night. And they're talking about keeping me here!" She tells me she will not be able to see me in that case. As a psychologist, she has no visiting-doctor privileges. She tells me we can talk on the phone, though, and she has Dr. F. call me to report what she knows of the doctors' plans for me. When Dr. F. calls, I ask her about St. Elizabeth's. "It's the public mental institution in DC," she answers.

No wonder Judy used St. Elizabeth's as a threat. Public services are not the District's strong point.

"When I spoke to the doctor and the social worker," Dr. F. continues, "I told them I simply will not stand for your being sent to St. E's. That's called patient dumping and you have a right to pay however you choose. If they bring up St. Elizabeth's again, threaten to sue."

Somehow I don't feel up to this. I'm still groggy and now I'm more depressed than I was this morning. But I simply won't be controlled. I won't let them cart me off like a piece of trash.

I begin looking around the room for ways to die. I could drown myself in the toilet, maybe even in the sink. The window looks unbreakable. I picture myself diving out of a vehicle if they try to transport me to St. Elizabeth's, sprinting down the street barefoot, in my skimpy hospital gown.

As I contemplate my escape, my head begins to throb with anger. The nurses deceived me when they told me they wanted my valuables for safekeeping. Unless they suspected the sitter, they knew no one could steal anything from my room. I'm being watched every second. They took only those items they thought would help me escape: my license, my credit cards, my cash, my checkbook, and my house keys. No wonder they didn't want my student library card. My throat tightens with disgust as I remember my naiveté, my complicity in stripping myself of my freedom: *there's sixty dollars in my coat.*

Late at night, a young, handsome doctor visits. He asks me why I took the pills and I explain.

"But why couldn't you take just one pill?"

I explain again, more slowly.

He still looks unsure, but has a list of questions to get through. He asks me what I want to do now, and I tell him I want to go home and finish the semester, that I'm in a master's program.

He looks at me for a moment. "You're an *educated* person and you did this!"

I'm stunned. Virginia Woolf, Vincent van Gogh, Sylvia Plath, Marina Tsvetaeva, John Berryman, Ernest Hemingway, and an endless stream of other writers and artists were well educated when they killed themselves. "Yeah, well, I didn't study chemistry."

He stares. "Well, I guess even intelligent people do stupid things sometimes."

I hear the voices of my next visitors at 6:00 a.m. but keep my head turned toward the wall. The blond doctor calls my name. She is standing in a line with three others, one of whom is the handsome twerp.

"Sorry to wake you up. We're making our rounds and I wanted to let you know that we haven't found a psychiatrist who will evaluate you yet and it may be late afternoon before we do."

I stifle a groan.

"Have you had anything to eat since you've been here?"

"No. Except for the charcoal."

The doctors laugh and exchange glances, as if to say, "See, she's not depressed." Humor and extreme civility are my only weapons.

My humorous facade is difficult to maintain, however, and when a nurse strides into my room and begins busying herself with my chart, my sense of humor fails.

"Did they give you charcoal?" she asks with a bright smile.

"Yes."

"So is your poop black?"

"No," I scowl.

"Oh, then I guess you're digesting it," she laughs, breezing out of the room.

I begin to understand the pattern: I'm an inferior being here, a person who didn't try hard; a person who does stupid things; a person who can be ribbed cavalierly by a stranger about the color of her poop—if I'm a person at all. I suspect I'm merely a source of income, susceptible to being bludgeoned with threats whenever payment is in question. All the psychiatrists who have been called and who have refused to see me and risk not getting paid—are they in the *helping* profession? I am thankful for the sitter. At least she credits me with a soul.

At last, I learn that a psychiatrist will be evaluating me around 11:00 a.m. I run a comb through my scraggly hair. I haven't showered in two days, I have yellow circles under my eyes from the Percocet, my eyelids are swollen from tears and lack of sleep, and I have no makeup. The psychiatrist is going to see what a wreck I am. They'll keep me here for weeks.

As I sit up on the bed and prepare to be animated and cheerful, a tall gray-haired man calls to me from the doorway, introducing himself. "May I come in?" he asks, waiting for me to answer. I love him already.

He understands why I wouldn't want to report this hospital visit to my insurance. "I was in analysis for a year," he confides, easing himself into the chair beside me, "and then I had the worst trouble getting insurance."

I run through the issues that underlay the overdose. When I tell him about the man who dumped me, he says the words that give me my first true smile in weeks:

"Well, I'd say he missed out."

The evaluation takes ten minutes. "You seem to be doing very well," he says. "I see no reason why you can't go home."

I have never been so ecstatic.

The ecstasy was expensive: two thousand dollars and twenty-one hours of terror. But it could have been more costly still. I was lucky to have found a psychiatrist who would see me and to have had Dr. F. to fight for me.

In spite of the costs, my hospital stay and what had precipitated it were useful in some ways. My therapist now allows me total control over decisions regarding antidepressants. She has promised to take me at my word always so that I won't have to resort to dramatics, and she has made a commitment to overestimating instead of underestimating my level of depression. I have promised to express my feelings as clearly as possible and to make a point of discussing problems instead of acting out. I now know I have to work out my abandonment issues before getting into another relationship. I've learned that if I ever get that depressed again, I should check myself into the best hospital around *before* making a suicidal gesture. Preferably I'd do that with a friend in tow. And I'd make damn sure whoever it is just happens to be a lawyer.

Since You Asked, Here Is Why

Amy Stuber

Lila walks like light on water, skittish as a moody ghost. She is a bird fleeing the gun.

"There are so many eyes," she has told me. "It feels like they're always following me, watching. It feels like I am under constant visual assault."

I sense that in real life she would not reveal as much. But we are in a hospital, a laboratory setting, where such emotional experiments are encouraged.

Her foot steps are moth wings on flannel. She weighs eighty-two pounds. She screams and cries five times her size every evening when they make her drink the milky canned dietary supplement. They talk to her in watered-down candy voices, soft and easy to swallow. The more abrasive she becomes, the smoother they grow, chilled silver. The nurses are human food processors: efficient, clucking, whirring. They treat her like a baby. That is what she has become. She will not feed herself. She likes hunger grinding away at her organs. Her body, for lack of another substance, is consuming itself. She likes this. She has told me so, and I know.

She is regressing. Soon she will lie in a ball as if returning to the womb, will lose her voice and only moan. She will grow infantile. And then she will cease to grow at all.

Before I was brought here by my parents, with their heads full of question marks, I ate only two things for some time: broccoli and steamed rice in near thimble portions. And then that felt like too much. So I ate only sugarless gum, one stick three times a day. Until I fainted in the shower and cut my head open, and my roommate called my parents three states away to come get me. I remember feeling relieved.

Lila is my second roommate to commit slow suicide, refusing to get better. The first was sent to intensive care. And for a time the room was mine alone. I slept in the bed by the window on even days and the bed by the door on odd ones until the nurses reprimanded me for creating extra work by messing up two beds instead of one.

But now Lila lies still like night snow in the bed next to me, her body barely denting the mattress. Sometimes she cries when she thinks I'm sleeping. But I know not to say anything.

If I were a nurse or a doctor, if I worked here, I would scoot onto the edge of her bed and ask: "Are you okay? What's wrong, honey? Why don't you tell us what's bothering you?" But I don't say anything because I know why she is shrinking. She is tired of being seen.

When I want to take a shower, I have to go to the nurse's station and tell them. If I want to shave my legs, I have to check out a razor, for five minutes. If I stay longer, one of them comes in to check on me. If I want to leave, I must apply and receive permission. I can only leave on Saturdays and Sundays between ten and five for three hours at a time. And I must be escorted by a family member. If I want to go out by myself or with a friend, the time is shaved down to two hours. For exercise, I am allowed to walk up and down the halls three times a week for thirty minutes at a time. I can only make phone calls between seven and ten at night and they cannot exceed the fifteen-minute time limit. I must talk about how I feel during group sessions. If I am asked a question by one of the psychiatrists during group, I must respond, if only to say, "I don't feel like talking right now." I cannot lose weight. These are the rules.

It is morning but still dark. In the bed next to mine, Lila does sit-ups under her blanket, watching the door to make sure she is not caught. She does these things in the morning, in her bed: sit-ups, leg lifts, arm circles. Sometimes I can feel her looking at me, like she is trying to enlist me in this routine. But I keep my eyes closed and listen.

I can hear Eleanor, one of the night nurses, shuffling down the hall. She starts and stops, halting at every door to deposit two star-speckled gowns on the vinyl chair in every room. This is the last of her nightly duties. Then she will collapse on the fraying green sofa in the smoking room and have a cigarette before she goes home. I have been here three months now, so I know the routine. I can identify action by sounds.

This is what we do every morning at six o'clock: weigh in like some meager bunch of wrestlers attempting to reach our weight. The floor is cold linoleum but we cannot wear socks, only flimsy gowns because they know how much each weighs: three ounces.

Lila trails behind me. Her lips have the blue-green cast of weathered copper. Her bones look sharp beneath her skin. The regularity of this event does not decrease its misery. We are all close to tears as we approach the scale. But Lila looks smug, chalky, and indifferent. She has not gained weight. She knows her body as she will know nothing else.

I put my feet on the icy metal, watch as the nurse toys with the markers. She steadies the balance and then records the numbers in her notebook. "Ninety-four! That's great. Only eleven more to go and then you can think of getting out of here." She smiles, pushing her brown bangs away from her eyebrows. I cringe and step away with my head down. I hear the thud and clang of the scale as it settles and returns to zero. Nothing.

Lila lifts her feet onto the scale. They are fragile as glass. The nurse frowns. "Lila, it looks like you're down to eighty-one. Dr. Price will not be happy to hear that. And you know that means we're going to have to give you more supplement or an IV, one of the two." But Lila isn't listening. And she isn't attempting to hide her pleasure. She is a child on Christmas morning. She is beaming, having won the prize. If she can control nothing else, she will control her body. She will mold and shave until she is pure bone. She wants to be that good, that pure.

I have started eating because I am tired of fighting with everyone. On Monday mornings, a small straight-haired teenage girl drops off two menus on the rolling table in between our beds. On purple and white pages, the meal options are listed. We have been told to make healthy choices. The fact that we are given menus, given the chance to select our fare for every meal every week, is something of a false front: If I circle "Fruit Plate" for each lunch and dinner, as I did my first three weeks, the dietician will return the menu to my room with a yellow Post-it note attached to the top that says, "Ha ha. Nice try. How about some variety?"

The dietician has informed me that it is imperative for me to experiment with my food selection. She said it just like that. So I try. To impress her, I order the steak sandwich for Tuesday's dinner. And then I end up pushing the food around over every spot of my plate. But the nurses are experts at this game. One of them positions herself at the door like a warden. You must pass by her, like a customs agent, before sliding your tray back onto one of the food carts. And half of the food that originally rested on the plate must be gone. So I force some of it down, enough to convince her that I have eaten. Afterward, I sit in the lounge staring at the TV, feeling like a balloon. I want to throw up, stick my fingers down my throat. But they lock the bathroom doors, all of them, after every meal.

Lila doesn't even bother with the menus. She circles nothing, returns the sheet unmarked. So they give her the fruit plate because they think she might eat fruit if nothing else. She cuts the cantaloupe into tiny pieces and shovels them into her napkin, then throws the wad into the trash when the nurse is busy examining someone else's plate. Later, she sits next to me in the lounge, tight and perfect and contained. I look at her, her feet close together, her hands pinned to her lap, a thoroughly compact package. I feel like I'm oozing, running out of my boundaries. How much space am I allotted? I am sure that I am taking more than my share.

Twice a week I see a psychiatrist. When he sits in his leather chair his feet barely graze the floor. He is the sort who asks questions and continues speaking without waiting for an answer. He seems to have grown accustomed to little or no response.

"Do you see a pattern involving negative feelings surrounding food in your family?" he asks. "Do you think this is something that has evolved through the generations? Do you think other members of your family have perhaps assuaged their anxieties through the use of eating disorders as distraction, or a device for numbing emotion?"

Yes, I think to myself. But I don't say this. I don't want to give him anything.

On Tuesday mornings we have body image class. We have to wear tight-fitting clothes, as tight as we can find. In leotards and swimsuits and T-shirts, we parade down to the first floor. Led by a counselor, we enter the room that has been set aside for the cardiac patients, a room with various exercise machines and floor-to-ceiling mirrors covering the walls. We are given time to use this room once a week for three hours. We huddle in a semicircle around one set of mirrors. One at a time, we are supposed to approach our own reflections and name three positive parts of our physical selves.

"If you can't think of three, at least name one," the counselor instructs.

People lie. "I like my ankles," someone says. And then she says, "No, not my ankles, my wrists." Then she squirms away. We hate to like ourselves. Any small piece of self-acceptance might be interpreted as ego, as conceit.

When I go to the mirror, I look at the borders of my body. They blur as I stare. The counselor taps her pencil on her clipboard. "I know you can think of something," she says. "Come on, try to set an example for the newcomers."

"Okay, I like my ears," I tell her. She sighs. I pull my T-shirt back over my bathing suit.

When everyone has had a turn we are told to lie on the floor. The counselor turns the lights down and starts a relaxation tape, something about counting backward and taking an elevator. I watch the chests around me rise and lower. When the tape ends, we follow our leader out the door. I forget, until Tuesdays, about the rest of the hospital. But when we leave our wing and venture out into the sea of stares that inevitably greets us as we walk through the lobby, I remember how sick we all look.

Lila is not the worst. She is simply the worst that I know best. But there are others, a real freak show. Once a woman in the elevator turned to me and asked questions, trying to make sense of us. "Dear, you look fine, too skinny even. Why are you doing this to yourself?" Then the doors opened and I was saved from having to respond.

I thought about it later. I wanted to say something. I wanted to explain to the woman on the elevator the separation between mind and body. I wanted to tell her that, on one level, I knew. But that all the same, I had created something inside myself which I couldn't restrain. I doubted she would understand.

On Tuesday nights we gather around the locked doors of 4 East. At seven o'clock a nurse opens the doors and begins allowing visitors to enter. Another nurse wheels out a silver cart full of chocolate chip cookies, the wide flat pancake kind, and a jug of lemonade, along with paper cups and paper towels for napkins. Most of us walk around the food but never actually touch it.

My parents come in. My father looks at the floor, dragging his feet. He is like a child on his first day of school. My mother, smiling broadly, bounds forward. We have been through this ritual more than twenty times. My mother takes a cookie and nibbles around the edges. She doesn't want to suggest she has any problems around food. She wants to be clear that my problem isn't her fault. She asks me about my friends here, about activities, and groups. She doesn't stop looking at me. My father does not look at me at all. He keeps his eyes on his hands, lifting them occasionally to glance out the window. When my mother says his name, snapping her fingers to get his attention, he shudders as if grazed by a bullet.

I look over at Lila and her mother. Their movements are vague and gentle. They complement each other as if they are one delicate being.

I look at my parents again. The three of us seem at odds, like we are tied together at the center but all wilting in different directions. I want to pull my arms and legs into my abdomen and hear only the sound of silence.

When they are gone, I sit by the window and watch the rain as it starts hitting the pavement. The silence has the texture of sandpaper. It has expectations, corners to fill. It is not as smooth as I expected.

After my release from the hospital, I do not return for a year. I cannot bear the memory of myself in those halls and rooms. I am told to come back at least once a week for outpatient treatment. But I am determined, in this as in all other ventures, to succeed on my own. I do call after three weeks, however, while I am doing well, to ask about Lila. She has been transferred to intensive care, I'm told; she is being fed intravenously.

I move to the city and find a job as assistant to a company vice president. I remain careful, obsessive about food. I count and weigh. I cannot eat in restaurants because I don't know how they prepare the food. I maintain my weight at one hundred pounds. In some ways, I am better. I can live in the world.

When I go home for Christmas, I return to the hospital. All the same bodies wearing different faces roam the halls, sit in the lounge, lie flat on the beds. In the room I once shared with Lila, there are family pictures on the walls above the bed. Helium balloons float from the metal bedframe. One of the nurses recognizes me. I ask her about Lila, who still haunts me with her blue-ribbon scale smirk. The nurse says she remembers Lila's mother checking her out. "I think she transferred to another hospital closer to home," she says.

Lila's existence is a question. I think she might appear someday, on the street, on the bus, in the doorway of my office. With her whisper steps, I would not hear her approach. I would simply look up and she would be standing there, small and precise, her stare as loud as bombs.

Death Interrupted

Barbara Shooltz Kendzierski

I live a Lazarus life,
a death interrupted,
foiled by effective
intervention.

The resident on call dictates:
Formulation—conflicts
involving desire to die,
yet longing to live.

We make a pistachio cake
in OT today. Six of us
take turns folding
Jell-O pudding into Cool Whip.

Later in group,
they tell us to be positive
and assertive but not aggressive,
then lead us to the dayroom for meds.

I hear the click
of double doors
at the corridor's end
locking the world out.

Two frightened student nurses
ask me to play Scrabble.
How can I explain
the words have all been used?

Outstanding Charges

Barbara Shooltz Kendzierski

Habib, you shocked me
thirteen times indifferent
to the price I might pay.
You floated into my head
on your cloud of authority
in your hand-tailored suit
and monogrammed shirt.
Disguised in warm soothing words
you promised to be worthy
of my faith in you.
Then in my darkness
you stripped me
when I said I was bright
and you scoffed, *merely fair*
by my standards—
so little to lose
from your point of view.
I needed to believe
so I seized
what you offered and fell naked
into the electric grasp
of your manicured hands.
You milked my brain dry
then shrugged when your cure
did more harm than good.
With a laugh you tossed
out your words as you tossed
out my trust pronouncing yourself
much too busy to see me again.
You profited handsomely
from your promise broken.
But Habib, you were wrong
about me.

The Setup

Mary Hower

The hospital sign was missing letters. Doctor's Offices had become D TOR OFF. Was it falling apart or not quite set up?

My parents, my husband, and I were met by a nurse. "What brings you here?" she asked. I tried to talk but couldn't.

"I don't want to be here," I finally said.

My parents looked at their shoes.

"No one really wants to go to the hospital, but sometimes it's necessary," said the nurse. Earlier that afternoon, the psychiatrist had said the same thing.

Again I was silent. My father and my husband (M.) left the room. My mother stayed with me.

"I'm afraid, I guess."

"This isn't like *One Flew Over the Cuckoo's Nest,* you know."

I nodded. But no, I didn't know.

She'd given me a piece of paper titled "Patient's Rights." I could read it, phrases anyway. Little snatches assured me that if I could sign myself in, I would be voluntary. Not held against my will.

M. came back in the room, held my hand.

"Do you want to try it a few days?" the nurse asked, coaxing me.

I signed the form. She took me to my room and began going through my belongings. M. had packed my bag hours before, crying. In addition to my clothes, he'd packed a decoration we'd had in the apartment, a stuffed blue and silver paintbrush made of glittery material, white strings for the bristles. "Not a teddy bear," he said, "but it will have to do." The nurse looked at the stuffed paintbrush quizzically, then rummaged through my wallet, extracting money and credit cards. "You won't need these while you're here," she said, and gave them to M. I didn't know why I was being searched, why I was being invaded. She left the room while I said goodbye to M. with tears in his eyes again.

After my parents and M. left, the nurse returned, asked if I would like to see the ward. She showed me the dayroom with the ping-pong table and the television, showed me the refrigerator. Inside were cartons of Jell-O, fruit, and little portions of leftovers, Post-it notes attached with patients' names written on them.

"This is Bette," the nurse said, introducing me to an old woman who shook and smiled when she said hello.

The showers were locked. If we wanted to take one, we had to ask.

"And this is your roommate." A large woman with bald patches on her head was lying in bed.

"What are you in for?" she asked me when the nurse left.

"I don't know. What should I do?"

She sighed. "I guess you'll just have to ask your doctor about that."

Dr. G. came into my room the next morning and said he wanted to examine me. I felt embarrassed as I lifted my hospital gown. The morning nurse and a student nurse looked on as witnesses. He pressed in the area of my uterus. When he was finished, the morning nurse asked, "How long are you going to be here?" I said I didn't know and she looked at me crossly.

The dayroom was the color of Tang and was filled with blue-gray cigarette smoke. The lighter was bolted to a large white post in the middle of the room, sparking just enough to light a cigarette. Everyone smoked except a few of us, and when I asked about the policy a few days later, my hair and clothes reeking of smoke, I was told that since there were very few freedoms left to the patients, smoking was permitted.

The first day, I was given a pill in a white cup, then taken to the occupational therapy room. The therapist showed me the kinds of crafts I could make: a tooled keychain or bookmark, a tiled coaster, a wood-burning project, a crocheted hat. She suggested I start with a trivet, since it was the easiest of the projects. She gave me the printed instructions on how to make it as well as a form to fill out. After each step was completed, I was instructed to stop and answer a question on the form. I quickly became confused. "What is your typical schedule?" the question read and asked me to fill out a weekly plan. Since I had just left school, I didn't have a schedule anymore. I decided to write in the old one I'd had last year at school: wake, study, eat, study, eat, study, sleep. It felt like a test I couldn't pass, and I left the form halfway filled out, with only a few tiles glued to my trivet.

That evening, my parents came. We were allowed to go to the cafeteria, and I asked them why they were angry at me, and they told me they weren't. "Please don't make me stay here," I cried. My father took me by the hand and led me back to the ward.

Day three began on the same unvarying schedule. Before 7:00 temperatures were taken and pulses were charted in the darkness before breakfast. We dressed and showered from 7:00 to 7:30. No gowns could be worn out of one's room, and shoes, not slippers, must be worn at all times. At 7:30, breakfast was brought in on a warming table, and we were to serve ourselves, cafeteria style. No one was permitted to stay in their rooms to sleep or lie down. The schedule included pills in the morning, followed by the doctor's morning rounds. I saw Dr. G. for fifteen minutes each day, followed at 10:00 by occupational therapy in the crafts room. At 11:00 everyone met in one of the "classrooms" for group therapy. Lunch was at noon, followed by recreational therapy in mid-afternoon, which meant an outing for those with off-ward privileges. If not, there was an indoor activity, a medications class where you learned about what pills you were taking, or shuffleboard. Dinner at 5:00, then community meeting or bingo. Visiting hours were at 7:00, then a sleeping pill and bedtime.

At first, I told myself that I wasn't in a mental hospital. It was, I reasoned, the psychiatrists' "real" office, not the phony one I'd been taken to by my parents. It was a clinic where people were treated for the day and went home with their families at night. In the morning, after a drug-induced deep sleep, "they" were all there again, assembled like a cast of characters. I had an explanation for who they were—not really patients, but volunteers from my parents' church who were holding me hostage because I'd gone AWOL from Catholicism. They were there to bring me back or to teach me a lesson.

"*Who are you?*" I finally demanded during my third group therapy session. I'd been silent, but I could stand it no longer.

The only one who answered was a crew-cut man in his mid-fifties. "I'm a father, a husband, a son," he said. "I was laid off my job, had twenty-five years in with the company. . . ." Afterward, a young African-American woman came up and embraced me. "Don't worry, honey, if it's only your first time here. It's my third."

After my unsuccessful attempt at unmasking them, I distanced myself, watching, saying very little, overhearing them talk. Complaints about heart trouble, wrecked cars, illness. So many excuses!

From my bed one morning, I heard two young women walking by my room, laughing. I thought I heard one of them mock me. "I'm here because it's better than creative writing."

I was there because anything else would have been too easy. Real jail wouldn't have been enough. I thought I could run away, but the church volunteers were showing me that no matter where you run, people know who you are. People see the fake you are. People know you tried to run out on your life—your commitments, family, church. And you couldn't just run back, they were saying, couldn't just run back when it seemed convenient. You had to face up to things, you had to face up to people you'd run out on. Even if the people didn't know you, they knew, word got around. You couldn't just leave your parents, tell everyone how horrible they were, how horrible your religion was, then run back to them expecting help. People saw through that, no matter where you were. And these people were friends of my parents, and they were going to stand up for what was right. This was my punishment. This was like the boy Sister Elizabeth told us about in first grade, the boy who said he hated what his mother gave him to eat at dinner. Then he was taken prisoner in a war, fed bread and water. "This serves me right," the boy said. Just as this served me right.

"I don't have a feeling that this is really real," I said to the nurse, the one with the blond hair and the kind face.

I got out my little tray with the trivet I'd started the day before and searched for the instructions. Today I'd concentrate on the trivet. But I couldn't find the instructions.

"Someone's taken the instructions from my storage tray," I told the blond nurse.

"Someone?"

I nodded.

"Well, then I guess you'll have to ask me what to do."

But she was off then, helping someone else. I waited for her to come back, then approached her. "I'll be with you in a second," she said. Finally, ten minutes before the session was over, she came back. "What do I do next?" I asked. She looked at the clock. "You have to go to that box and find some tiles, but the time's almost up. I guess you can do it tomorrow." Another punishment.

In group therapy, I decided to test my theory that they'd blocked out the real programs on TV and put in tapes that looped continuously. "You've done something to the television," I told the nurse. It wasn't part of the script she had written for the daily group session, and she drew a sharp breath. "Why would we do something to the television? Why would we hurt you?" she asked, tensely.

After that, I was silent during group. An old woman in one session said she was in the hospital because her husband had died and she was depressed. Then she looked down at her hands and began crying. I knew she wasn't faking it, just as I knew that the Vietnamese girl in the room down the hall was also crying real tears. "It's okay to cry," I had heard the nurse comfort her. "You've been through some horrible things."

But what had happened to me was nowhere near losing a loved one or growing up in a war-torn country. I'd been the victim of a break-in, but I wasn't harmed and nothing much was taken. But somehow over the ensuing month, I'd fallen apart and had to leave school. Nothing that bad, so why did I feel this way? Was I faking it? Why didn't it feel quite real?

V., a woman in her late thirties, seemed real to me. Her voice shook when she said she was there because she was the sole support of her family and she had lost her job. I felt comfortable with her, played rummy even though I kept forgetting how. "It's okay," she assured me. I watched as she drew trees in art therapy, trees without leaves on their branches, winter trees.

One day, S., in his mid-twenties, a guy with long dark hair who played random notes on the piano, chords that sounded good by themselves but didn't add up to anything, came by the table where I was sitting. He was chain-smoking as usual.

"Are you an artist?" he asked.

"No, why?"

"You look like an artist."

Another day, he came by and asked, "What do you want to do?"

"What do you mean?"

"I mean: there's a bench down by the river, and trees. I mean: don't you want to get out of here, go down there?"

My mother thought he was creepy. "What's wrong with him?" she'd whisper hoarsely as he passed. A funny thing happened to S. during visiting hours. He'd start acting strange, circling tables at random, seeming disoriented. When everyone left, he'd stop, come back into focus. "I don't think anything's wrong with him," I said to my mother.

"Oh, yeah." She rolled her eyes.

S. and I had "chair exercises" together, which consisted of twirling strips of torn white cloth in the air and bending over to touch our toes. Two student nurses led the exercises, passing each other looks, barely able to suppress laughter. Were they making fun of us? I looked around at the other faces, all of them impassive. Afterward, I asked S.: "Didn't you think that was stupid?"

"I don't think anything is stupid," he said.

When I wasn't feeling mocked, I was feeling terrified. The three old women who had begun the week playing cards, one by one began to sit listlessly at the table. I was alone with one of them as she began to cry and shake, putting her head in her hands. I saw bruises on her arms. Bette came by and sat down with her. "It's all right. Did you start the treatments yet?" My first thought was, beauty treatments? Then I knew it was code for electroshock.

There were worse wards than the one I was on. On the sheet they'd handed out when I was admitted, I read that on the stricter ward, you could have flowers, but they had to be behind bars in a little space in the wall. At the worst, you'd be in the rooms where you couldn't have flowers at all. I looked across the hospital courtyard to a wall where there had been four windows. They were bricked in now, the newer brick lighter in shade than the old. Was that where the rooms stripped bare of anything were, where you couldn't even have flowers behind bars? Was that where they had put the teenage girl who wore pink pants and ate standing up next to the warming table, the girl who had disappeared into "isolation"?

Something was happening to my body that was hard to explain. I couldn't sit without jumping up and having to walk around. I didn't tell anyone for days. Finally, the up-down-up routine became more than I could bear. Sweating heavily, I told the nurse, who seemed alarmed. "I'll tell your doctor," she said, and a little later returned with my pills.

"He's changed your prescription," she said. Up until then, I'd been taking what I thought were placebos. No one had explained what they were for. Then I noticed how hard it was to urinate, and a few days later, to defecate. I sat in the bathroom counting tiles, knowing I had to pee, but not being able to, ashamed for having lost this kind of control, and not wanting to tell anyone.

One day I looked up at the little blackboard above the nurse's station and saw my name with "Preg Test" written next to it. I hadn't had sex with M. for two months.

"Am I getting a pregnancy test?" I asked the nurse.

She consulted my chart. "I guess so." Then she sat down with me, leaned over to invite my confidence. "How would you feel if you were pregnant?"

"I don't think this is a very good time for that, do you?" I replied.

She stood abruptly. "Only you can decide that, I guess."

Two days later, my period came. What was I to do? I wadded up toilet paper. When my mother came, I whispered it to her.

"Did you tell the nurse?"

"No—was I supposed to?"

"Well, why not? You're always supposed to tell the nurse when you're in the hospital."

At medications class the nurse said, "This is to help you understand what medications you are currently taking and how to take care of any side effects." Then she guided us through a filmstrip. The mind was like a filing cabinet, one frame offered. A perky secretary stood in high heels about to open the cabinet. "But sometimes, things can get out of order." In the second frame, files popped out of the drawer, all askew. Lights back on, the nurse began to read off the common side effects we might be experiencing and what to do about them.

"Constipation? Have your doctor order you a mild laxative. Blurred vision? Don't read or watch television. Stiffness of muscle? Do mild stretching—our chair exercises are good for that. Urinary hesitancy? Make sure to drink plenty of water. Dry mouth? Sip a glass of water, chew gum, or suck on hard candies. Or ask your doctor to order you some saliva."

I woke up. *Order us saliva?* I began to laugh. All of the students sat in the classroom desks, nodding impassively. What was wrong with everyone?

After a while, I learned that if I wanted something, I had to "go through my doctor for that." This rule became clear on a beautiful October afternoon when the other patients got excited about an outing to the park. "Are you going?" everyone asked each other. Yes, I thought, of course I'm going. I've been stuck here a week without going out once. The recreation therapist called out names.

"You didn't call mine," I said from the back of the line.

"What's your name?" he asked, looking at his list. "No, you don't have off-ward privileges."

"What?"

"You have to go through your doctor for that," he explained, as the rest of the group took off.

I had been meeting with my doctor all week and he never mentioned anything about privileges. Now, when questioned, he simply said, "You're restricted to the ward."

"But why?" I asked. "Why can't I go out?"

"That's what I've thought best. I can write you a pass for two hours off ward in the custody of your parents. Would you like that?"

"I want to leave," I said.

"No, no. That wouldn't be a good idea."

Friday night, most of the rest of the patients left for family visits. I panicked. How would I make it through the weekend alone? I went to the phone. If my psychiatrist was real, he would be there. I found the P's, but the pages for psychiatrists were torn out. It was part of the set-up. They didn't want you calling a real psychiatrist. "Is something the matter?" the nurse called out from the station.

"I want to talk to my psychiatrist."

"What for?"

"I want to get out of here."

She checked my chart. "Your doctor's out for the next few days. Dr. J. is covering for him. I'll leave a message with his service."

The word covering seemed coded, as in "covering over" or "undercover agent."

"Dr. J. says he'll see you tomorrow."

Saturday morning dawned gray. The LPN came in to take my temperature and pulse, followed by Dr. J., who sat on my bed, the room dark in the predawn.

Dr. J. was in his sixties, and I'd never met him before, though I'd seen him making rounds. "You called me last night?"

"Yes."

"What did you want?"

"I don't want to be here. I want to go home."

"I see, and have you discussed this with Dr. G?"

"Yes."

"And what does he say?"

"He says he thinks I should stay."

"Well, then, I can't let you out. He has to do that."

I looked down.

"How old are you?" he asked, sitting on my bed, me still in my nightgown.

"Twenty-six."

"Is there anything else I can do for you?"

"I want to go outside."

He smiled, as if I'd said something funny. "Be sure to wear a raincoat."

My parents took me to the park. The leaves had begun to change color, squirrels hurrying to bury their nuts. Nuts. "I don't know why I'm here," I said again. I said it every time I saw them, and every time they didn't have an answer. "The doctor says you need to stay a little while."

The second week, they let me outside with a student nurse. She was twenty-one, newly engaged, starting nursing school. I felt old beside her, reminiscing about high school. "I was into everything. I had a lot of friends. I even ran for student council and won." Then I added, "I tried to commit suicide last month." It felt good to tell someone.

"Pills?"

"How did you know?"

"That's the way a lot of people do it," she said softly.

Back in the occupational therapy crafts room, I had advanced from making the trivet to tooling a key chain in leather cut in the shape of a cat's head. As I tooled the eyes of the face in, the therapist asked me about my cat.

"Do you miss him?"

"Yeah."

"What's his name?"

"Merce."

"Merce? That's a funny name."

"It's after Merce Cunningham, the modern dancer."

"Oh. Where do you live?"

"I was living in New York. Before that, I lived in California near San Francisco."

"Then why are you here?"

"This is where my parents live. When everything started . . . falling apart, I needed to live somewhere. I'll go back to California. Have you ever been there?"

"Just for vacation—I'd never want to live there."

Maybe *I'd* made the wrong choice. Maybe I should be like her, sane and living in the Midwest, enjoying the flat landscape. I painted the eyes of the cat open, thinking I'd sentenced him to be forever watchful.

"What did you do before coming here?" the therapist asked.

"I taught English to college freshmen and went to school."

"Do you think you'll get your old job back when you leave?"

"No." If she didn't know about the restrictions on teaching fellowships, I didn't want to explain.

"I'm not doing too well here, am I?"

The night nurse looked up from the notes she'd made on my chart. " 'Shows signs of dependency on others, suspicion, lack of appetite.' No, I guess you're not doing too well here."

How was I supposed to be? Like E., who sat, head tilted to one side, quiet, legs crossed, feet in slippers? Or like the large woman in her twenties with her hair shaved, who molded clay in OT and laughed, "It's aggression therapy," punching her fist in the pile of gray, turning it over, punching it again.

"I see that anywhere you are, there's a structure. There's a structure here."

Dr. G. wrote down anything I said in beautiful calligraphic script. He let me go out now for recreational therapy. I looked for signs of the setup. Someone had cut initials into their front lawn with their lawn mower, and I was sure it was a message for me. But in the woods the setup began to dissolve a little. The trees were real after all. Elms. Alders. Maples. They existed apart from me and would continue.

I saw a *Newsweek* in the dayroom. Everything I read or heard seemed made up. "Earthquake in Mexico Kills Thousands." "Those poor people still on the *Achille Lauro*." Another impossible story.

They showed a cartoon. "It has to do with Halloween. Ichabod Crane, the Headless Horseman." Ichabod taught, as I had done. In the cartoon, he was presented as a bucktoothed nitwit. Slowly, my face grew hot, my humiliation increasing; surely they had shown the cartoon to make fun of me. I ran from the room. The nurse said, "I guess she didn't like it."

Like a fever breaking, I finally glimpsed something I thought was real. I'd gone to bed but hadn't fall asleep right away. Outside my room, I heard laughter. I tiptoed out to see all the patients grouped around the TV watching the World Series. It hit me, mid-October. I watched for a moment with them, cheered by the reality of a baseball game.

Finally, the tears flowed. In my room where I sneaked alone time, I sobbed quietly, able to touch my feelings again. A nurse I hadn't seen before heard me and sat down on the bed. "Why are you crying?" she asked.

"I don't know why. I dropped out of school. It feels like I've left everything behind, let everyone down." These were the first words I'd spoken in two weeks that made any sense.

"But you can always go back. I just heard about a lady who got her degree when she was seventy." She looked at me with tears in her eyes.

My grandmother brought me books about Ireland, where she grew up, talked to me as if I were a normal person. "My father was a fisherman, you know. I used to wait for him to come back home. Can she go to the cafeteria?" she asked the nurse. When the nurse said no, she said, "Did I ever tell you about how mean the nuns were? Once, one got so mad at me she came over and pulled my earlobe until it tore." She played rummy, asked me to hold her arm, and help her walk to the door.

"Please, just let me go home for the weekend," I asked the doctor.
"What will you do?"
"Cook dinner, read my niece and nephew a story."
"Do you still have the feeling that things are set up?"

I thought back to the trees, the baseball game, my grandmother, the nurse that cried with me. "Not all the time. When I do, I tell myself that they're not." He gave me permission for the evening.

Later, drawing up discharge papers, the nurse wrote "Depression" as the diagnosis. It was the first time I knew why I'd been hospitalized. Knowing, at last, made it real.

The Scream

J. Lisa Richesson

July 23

It is the black dog, the shroud, the creature that stalks your sleep. It rises out of mists on the moor and haunts your soul. It turns ordinary items into objects of terror. It forces you to cut deep straight lines down the inside of your arms, then you weep with relief for a focusing pain. Because the pain, the real pain, is psychic and ethereal, terrifying and inescapable. You cannot stop crying. You hyperventilate. You feel the crushing, suffocating weight of the world.

I am writing this in the hospital, on the psych ward. It is my fourth admission in twenty years. I hold up pretty well most of the time. But this time, the load I've been carrying has worn me down and I can't do anything for myself anymore.

My chest is tight with anxiety, even after the intake and the precious administering of Xanax. I fell apart at my job, locking myself in my office and crying. I couldn't sleep at night; instead, I paced the house, wringing my hands, afraid to sleep because of the dreams. I was splitting, scratching, seething back and forth between the beaten-down adult, the defiant teenager, and the terrified, speechless child.

At intake, they asked me if I was suicidal. I said no, I just wanted to carve myself.

I told the psychiatrist that I dissociated and had done so for some years. He had an immediate physical reaction, as if I'd told him I like to eat kittens. "Oh," he said, "I'm not sure I understand that."

Oh, Jesus, I thought. A nonbeliever.

"Well, let's see if I can help you to better understand the condition while I am here," I offered.

It's almost time for bed. The Xanax is beginning to work. I feel my breathing slowing down, the tightness in my chest lessening. I want to sleep now and be lifted by angels to happy places, to walk on clouds and spin ether through my hair.

July 24

Dream: I am visited by the psychiatrist. He is decked out in a Santa Claus cap and beard, but otherwise he is naked and his nipples are pierced. He gets into bed with me. I think, "Now, what am I supposed to endure?" He rapes me with a flashlight.

The scene dissolves. A black woman says, "You use that on me, I'll beat the shit out of you." I assume she is referring to the flashlight.

Breakfast comes. Funny how easily you fall into the rhythm of life in the hospital. My blood sugar is low, my blood pressure uncharacteristically high. Medications are given. The nurse, Margie, asks me to think about how to spend my day. All I want to do is sleep, now that I can, but I know that is frowned upon. I'm to report to team meeting in less than an hour with my plan for the day.

The night before coming here I had a huge panic attack. I felt death all around me. M. spoke to the room, banished the evil spirits, told me how vulnerable I am.

Besides the depression, I look at my surroundings and feel I could be anywhere: Pittsburgh; Margate on the North Sea; Holland. I don't recognize the familiar and have looked at M. in the middle of the night and wondered who she was. Dr. Hall says this is depersonalization, a puffed-up word to describe the fact that I am stressed to bursting.

As I lay in the hospital bed, with the blanket tucked around me and the sleeping pill taking effect, my thoughts stray randomly. I think about being fat all my life. When I was a trainee at the Post Office twenty years ago, new hires had to learn to drive vans. I remember how the seat belt barely fit around me, how when it popped off everyone laughed at me, including the instructor, and how it was perfectly OK to do that—to laugh at the fat person, to humiliate her.

July 25

In team this morning, I drop my facade. James, my beloved son, only weeks ago told me that he had been sexually abused by his father, and he thought I knew!

I tell the team my mind cannot grasp this. What kind of monster did I spend twenty-three years with? How could I have been so blind and stupid? How do I help my son heal? How do I forgive myself? I am so tired, so depressed.

This evening James calls, confused about why I am here. "Is it about me?" he asks. It's about a lot of other things, I tell him. He says he's forgiven me and I start to cry. But I haven't forgiven myself, I tell him. I don't know how.

Afterward I am tearful and agitated. The nurse comes in and suggests I write out a problem I'd like to change. How do I eradicate incest from my son's life?

Later . . . I check out two books from the inpatient library. Someone writes, "what [mental health professionals] don't understand is the fear involved in making any decision." That is how I lived all those years with Charles, abused, neither my son nor I knowing about the other. From *The Courage to Heal*, poet Muriel Rukeyser: "What would happen if one woman told the truth about her life? The world would split apart."

July 26

Group therapy this morning. Several members had just returned from ECT. They are docile, blank, momentarily relieved from intractable depression.

I am in a different place and time has stood still. Nothing is the same. I am not sure of anything. The ground on which I have walked for so many years has fallen away beneath me, yet I am not floating. I am free-falling on air thinned by lies and innuendoes.

Earlier, I met with Dr. Smoeller again. "How many, ah, personalities do you have?" he asked.

What is this? Sybil? I explained what it felt like to switch; the horrible, unique headache, the dizziness, the unreality. To satisfy his need for solid data, I told him I had three distinct personalities and that one was very destructive and had tried suicide many times. His eyes widened. He seemed genuinely concerned, but I longed to see Dr. Hall, who knows me so well and can bring out the Others so easily. I often hear my mother's voice telling me how stupid I am. Her voice drones, "You are making this up. There's nothing wrong with you. You are disgusting." Disdain and contempt ooze from her curled lips. I told Dr. Smoeller this and he ordered Zyprexa, an antipsychotic that may help with the voices and with organizing my thoughts.

July 27

There is so much anxiety this morning. It is difficult not to shake, not to want to scratch, not to become loud and aggressive. The nurse comes in and I tell her I've been very polite, compliant, cooperative up until now, but I can no longer guarantee my behavior. I can't promise her I won't hurt myself. I feel like screaming.

July 28

Dr. Smoeller seems to be catching on. He asks me about triggers and integration. I think he really cares. I tell him I am dredging for memories and events because I am tired of living this way, half a person. I am tired of fooling myself, tired of discounting my thoughts and intuitions and the plain facts.

There was abuse. I should have left, should have run barefoot in the night if necessary, but I didn't. Instead, I told myself every day that things would get better, that if we just got though the next months, just made it to the next year, the next blue moon, then everything would magically be better.

Now I dangle by one broken string. Dangle over a precipice, deep and dark. I hear screaming and it is my son, screaming for me. I dangle, reach for him, but cannot break the string. I float over him and his screaming gets louder and louder. I reach, but am pulled back. I cannot get to him.

I am putting these pieces of the puzzle together, working toward a wholeness I have not known since I was small, since I was in contact with my larger self, with the Universe. Dr. Smoeller tells me I need to find the answers to the following questions: How do I stop feeling guilty? How do I forgive myself? Where is my higher power?

I am relieved to have Dr. Hall call. She says I need a good screaming session. Such intriguing and different approaches; one cerebral, the other primal.

July 29

I want to be left alone today. Around me, patients are quietly beading (especially the ECT patients). Some are talking and painting pottery. I am using the computer again, although I suspect a quiet young man hanging out in the corner would like to play computer games.

I am looking for clues, and here is what I've found so far. I've written them so I can remember to tell Dr. Hall:

It's always been hard to trust my intuition.

I am often immobile, unable to make the simplest decision.

I have used my achievements at work to compensate for utter failure at home.

I have used food all my life to be big, to stuff things, to comfort.

I have hurt myself. I have cut my arms, overdosed on Valium and booze, drunk a bottle of ipecac, passed out while cooking and nearly burned the house down.

I do not know how to be angry. I either sublimate it completely or let it out in uncontrolled ways, ways that have been violent and abusive.

I sometimes hit my son. *I sometimes hit my son.* I've never said that out loud before. God, why can't you behave? Don't you know what will happen to you? To compensate, I protected him in other ways, surely unbalancing his own sense of reality.

I have never ceased to be amazed that people like me, that people even love me. I expect them to leave at any moment. I am an absolute expert in nonintegration. I can go to the ladies' room, break down in sobs, throw cold water on my face, and return to a business meeting as if nothing happened. My mother forced enemas on me.

July 30

Discharged home and into the Day Hospital program. I see Dr. Hall this morning. She tells me about narcissistic personalities. She says narcissists, for one reason or another, do not attach to someone else early in life; that we must all attach to someone, and in the absence of an appropriate person, young children attach to themselves.

August 1

Today in Day Hospital, after I have spoken, the nurse comments that I said some powerful things and she feels overwhelmed. She asks me how I feel. I don't feel anything. She says I need to feel my emotions, that I have spent my life not feeling, compartmentalizing. She's right, of course. How could I allow myself to feel my emotions? What would have happened if I had spoken about them, revealed the secrets? Would the world have split apart?

Diane, the nurse, talks about feelings, and how language defines us, how the words we use to express our feelings define us. Sadness becomes joy through language. What an intriguing idea.

August 2

Intense time today in Day Hospital. I find myself feeling enraged when a new patient talks about how her ex-husband told her she could come back any time she wanted. The arrogance of his statement just sets me off. After I spew about this in group, I am shaky and upset, tears close to the surface. I feel I am going to lose ground.

My anger scares me. It is powerful and tall, like a great cedar growing on a cliff above the ocean, battered by winds and storms. It is famous, celebrated, written about, discussed on talk shows. It is a volcano; the plume of ash is building and is about to explode, changing the landscape forever. The ash will spew for millions of miles. The weather will be perverse. Typhoons will blow through Paris. Rain will pelt the Sahara. The soil will change. Cucumbers will grow to the size of skyscrapers. One woman's anger will knock the earth off its axis and we will all reel in space, clinging to each other, stranger to stranger, needing each other, suddenly afraid.

"Good work," says Diane. "Good work."

August 3

What if I were to write my heart?

I immediately feel a scream forming in my chest. It almost reaches my mouth but I clench my teeth and hold it in. I feel screams rising up often. I have to bite my lip. Hard.

In a visit to the Day Hospital, Dr. Smoeller asks how I'm doing. Fine, I say. Except I have a barely controllable urge to scream. Maybe a small one, maybe just raise my voice a little higher. He advises against it unless I am in a therapeutic milieu.

Imagine it. Open your mouth. The scream starts from your toes, shoots past your knees, expands into your belly, gathers strength and volume in your chest. The pressure builds, your eyes bulge, your throat burns. And then it pushes past your esophagus, larynx. It fills your mouth with fire, your jaws explode and head flies apart and there it is. A scream so loud, so intense, so powerful that everything around you will stop and listen. No deaths. The only movement is the beating of your heart, which is stronger and clearer than it's ever been.

October

Dr. Hall encourages me, gives me the tools and mechanisms to go through with it. She says I am ready. I carefully pick a place, not too far from the city, but not too close either. I choose a wooded area with tall pines and aspens and cedars and Douglas firs.

I go alone, walking in slowly, sometimes seized with anxiety and trembling, other times enjoying the scent of the forest. When I reach my spot, I settle myself on some soft grass, surrounded by a grove of trees. I set out my water container, take a few sips. I talk to the trees. I tell them everything, in a rush, a torrent of words. I jump about in time and space, letting events unfold as they may. I tell them everything I can remember and the more I talk, the more I remember. The trees listen patiently, and I imagine that angels float above them.

Then, I begin to rock to and fro, gently, slowly, and when I have lulled myself sufficiently, I throw my head back and open my mouth. And out it comes, my breath coming in fast gulps, the suspension of breathing lengthening with each gulp. Louder and louder it becomes, longer and longer. I stand and stretch out my arms, and twirl.

The trees do not move, the grass stays still, the air fresh. The world stays the same, my scream a series of ever decreasing echoes. Yes, my world falls apart, I split open into a million tiny pieces. Now I am picking them up, placing them in a new order with each blessed new morning.

Hospital

Anne Myra Benjamin

I. FROM ONE SIDE OF THE WINDOW TO THE OTHER

It won't open.
On one side of the ward there is a locked, electric door.
On this side where I am standing
looking out into the street
my forehead presses against the iron lace
crowding the window
that won't open.
I am an Israelite
between the Egyptians
and the Sea.

I panic. I cannot
jump into the water to escape.
Only thousands of square holes
in the mesh over the window
through which to ebb my self
piece by piece, square by square
until I am—all of me—out.
Down in the parking lot
on the heliport
(where I have descended, parenthetically,
no one yet has noticed me)
where they piece together victims of major accidents
I sit, a pile of squares.

This time it is not the DSM-III or IV
that I use to remind me of how the pieces fit.
Instead, my daughter's DOT-TO-DOT book.
It is logical and not too many pages.
The picture I make is of a bear holding a balloon!

II. SIEGE

My friend Anna smoothed out the trash
on her lap "as good as new."
She never sat alone on the ward
but was always surrounded
by her bags: a barricade
of yoghurt tops and plastic 3cc medication cups
and cardboard toilet paper rolls
and empty and full sacks of saccharine
and tens of empty potato chip bags
and cheerful announcements
of events long past,
of bright, nearly blinding,
nursery school construction paper.

An art teacher
might have called this entourage
"Supplies."
The head nurse
called it "Insanity."
Never mind that beyond the walls
it had become most politically correct
for the upright to hoard Anna's artifacts
and call it "Recycling."
Every now and then,
you never knew exactly when,
the head nurse—without notice,
wordlessly threw out
Anna's line of defense.
Then I'd join this cyclical charade
to reinforce the ramparts with a contribution
from my collection of 7 oz. plastic cups.

III. CODE YELLOW

Late morning in the day room,
I am reading the Sports Section

(the rest of the paper is already stolen).
Something about a horse race
grows more opaque the more I read.
I feel sorry for the horses.
Then—hoofbeats! Is this the U.S. Cavalry,
come to deliver me?

Instead, forty human feet
burst through the locked front door,
—a nurse has dialed security.
A technician slams the door shut
and they crowd around
a ninety pound woman-child
who does not want to eat breakfast
force-fed through her nose.

It happens just as quickly
as the horse race in the paper.
The pandemonium is brief.
It is hard to see the action,
but in the end
my ninety pound friend
is tied to her chair
and the score is quite clear.

IV. Privilege Class

It's all in the timing.
Watch the doctor's lips.
Are they tightened or relaxed?
Don't look eager, Besides—
The charts say you do not deserve a favor.

If the doctor's lips are taut,
then tighten up your list,
You'll be sitting in this circle
next week and the next.

Listen to the whining
of the girl who lounges
in too prominent a chair,
a comic character.

Avoid the strident tone
you hear across the room
of the woman who demands,
"just wanna smoke whenever I want."

It's all in the timing.
That doctor is a stern taskmistress.
The centimeters on her ruler
either dilate or contract.

So even if you want an entourage
of faces from outside the walls,
"La Maitresse" may say you're "too psychotic"
to receive your calls.

Accept the news in silence.
Don't regret the minutes turned to weeks
of stashed away obedience that
should have added up to three Freedoms:
Smoking, Calling, and the Kitchen,

Impoverished now you gain a new gentility.
The schoolmarm cannot know how far
she's been surpassed, sitting uninvited
in the crowd of quiet faces.

Gather strength from silence.
This is your induction to Privilege Class.

Safe Places

Catherine Ann Fabio

I'm not hiding anymore. It's hard to create a life when you're hiding from something you can't even wholly name. Instead, I sit, and walk, and write, and sometimes even laugh in this other place, this little place with rickety chairs, and hanging plants and a yellow dog who breathes softly on my foot as I clickity click at my table, spilling words and memories onto the screen. I write from my heart and from my hands, and somehow, in the telling, my story retells itself, explaining to each part of me, reassuring me, as I come to understand, to make peace with myself and the world around me.

*   *   *

"Why are you here?"

I felt relieved to know the counselor wasn't speaking to me—not yet anyway. She was addressing another group member who had also, that day, entered the safe house for battered women.

Why are you here? I'd been asked that question so many times, and always when I was someplace I didn't want to be. The question was usually posed in a way that implied I was somewhere I wasn't supposed to be. In addition to feeling both defensive and ashamed, I always felt obligated to explain—and frankly, I'd run out of explanations.

Enveloped by a thick cloud of cigarette smoke, I half-listened to the conversation. Two women seemed to be doing most of the talking. The others didn't say anything. They just gazed down at the sticky wooden table or stared blankly across the room, holding their breath and then closing their eyes and breathing out long puffs of smoke. The video projectors in my head began to play, and I found myself splitting inside, watching and responding to each of them.

When I was a child, I did that a lot, created an interior world filled with images and voices that comforted me, especially when things became too chaotic or when I felt afraid. I'd close my eyes and go to that safe place inside my head and watch videos of summer camp. Eventually, I learned how to step inside the images; I could go to summer camp anytime I wanted.

This process of dissociating was an effective way to cope with the violence of my childhood—my father's beatings, my mother's angry rages. "Take it," my mother said once, pushing a butcher's knife toward me. "Take it, take it!" she shouted again and again. "Do us all a favor and kill yourself." Instead, I climbed the stairs to my room, closed the door, and retreated to that safe place inside my head. Summer camp.

There's a flip side to dissociation, however. Little did I know that while one of my mind's cameras focused on every detail of a safe or comforting experience—the perfume-and-coffee scent of my favorite camp counselor, the smack-crack sound of a baseball hitting a wooden bat—another camera was videotaping the violence, also capturing every detail—a paint-chipped radiator, an ornately carved table leg, the mildew odor of a damp cellar.

On my first night in the battered women's safe house, I couldn't seem to find any videos of camp, not even short clips. I could no longer get to camp—or anywhere safe—inside my head. Instead, I saw violent images from my past, scenes I thought I had escaped without seeing. They played on several projectors at once. And I couldn't look away.

"Catherine," a woman's voice interrupted my viewing, "why are you here?"

I looked up at the counselor, relieved to be distracted from the flashback.

"Catherine? Can you tell the group why you're here?"

I tried to turn off the movie, to shake off the shame, so I could focus on the counselor and the other women in the room. But the shame kept jumping back on me, kept flitting around me like annoying little gnats. And I kept shooing them away.

I knew she was expecting a response, but I didn't seem to have words, only pictures and feelings. The videos continued to play—a guard at the state hospital throwing a young woman on the floor while four other uniformed officers stripped her down to her underwear, dragged her into a quiet room, and threw her onto a mattress where they spread her legs and arms and strapped her down; me fishing tranquilizers from my mouth and hiding them in the seam of a red teddy bear; an eviction notice stapled to my front door; my suitcase and a box of Nancy Drew books on the driveway; a man driving his jeep with his left hand while he punched me with his right. Derrick.

I channel-surfed through the videos, pausing on the ones of Derrick. But the words just wouldn't come.

"Why are you here?" the doctor asked, looking up from the chart he was reading.

"Excuse me?"

"What are you doing here?" he demanded.

"They," I said weakly, pointing in the direction of the nurse's station, "they, um, told me to come in . . . "

"No!" the doctor said, waving his palm toward me, an amused smile crossing his face. "Here. This hospital."

"I didn't want to come," I stammered weakly. "I, I guess . . . I was depressed. . . . Is—isn't it in my chart . . . ?"

"Yes," he said, flipping through my chart, reading it like a grocery list, "major depression, bulimia, mood-congruent psychosis, occasional fugue states, self-mutilation, suicidal—"

I cringed with shame.

The doctor interrupted himself. "You're not going to get better here!" he said incredulously, tossing my chart on the desk.

I felt confused. "Well . . ." I began, "why . . . ? Why am I here?"

"Good question!" he exclaimed. "That's what I'd like to know."

I was unsure how to respond. Neither of us spoke. Then he took a deep breath and broke the silence.

"Basically," he said in a softer voice, leaning toward me with his hands clasped on the desk in front of him, "we're like a holding facility. We don't have the kinds of resources you need, individual psychotherapy, group counseling . . ."

"Why didn't somebody tell the doctors in Franklin Springs that?" I asked.

They knew, I silently answered myself.

He leaned back in his chair and sighed. "It's a matter of resources," he continued, speaking to me as if I were one of his colleagues. I liked that. It had been a long time since anyone spoke to me this way, kindly, expecting me to actually carry on a conversation requiring logic and reasoning.

They just wanted to get rid of us, I thought.

I knew some part of me was right about that. Suicidal patients are a liability. Nobody wants to lose a patient to suicide. How many doctors, psychologists, therapists had I been through before I finally realized that suicidal thoughts are not acceptable topics to discuss in therapy? I watched the faces of past therapists flash before me. How many of them managed to refer me to someone else—anyone else—whenever I tried to tell them about the suicidal yearnings? About how some parts of me can actually convince the rest of me that suicide is the best option? About the fear some parts of me have that I might actually carry it through? And how many sessions did any of them ever have with me after I tried to tell them about how I feel like I'm two or three or six or even eight people at one time? None. They usually changed my diagnosis to 301.83—borderline personality disorder—and then they dropped me, because, as one therapist put it, "Borderlines don't get better."

Yeah, an adolescent part of myself agreed; they didn't send us here so we could get better; they just wanted to get rid of us.

It made sense. Whether or not this place could help me was irrelevant. I was sent where suicidal people without insurance get sent. Linwood. The State Hospital.

The doctor confirmed my conclusion. "We basically keep people here to prevent them from harming themselves or someone else."

Yeah, right. I recognized the adolescent's voice, hoping it was only audible to me.

"People outside of here," he added quickly. Then he leaned forward again, looking me right in the eye. "This is a dangerous place for you."

Duh! she continued silently. I tried to pull her back, away from the doctor, and push the scholar part of myself forward.

I knew what he meant about danger. I'd only been there five days, and already I'd learned which hallways, which bathrooms, which patients and staff to avoid. And then, there was the matter of my roommates. Between their conversations about the nurses they fantasized about, the orderlies they'd "done it" with, and their comparisons of self-inflicted wounds, they talked idly of what they should do to me. Barely breathing, I lay in the dark, under a scratchy sheet, smelling the stench of Iona, the older woman in the next room, who couldn't or wouldn't control her bowels. I lay perfectly still, in the narrow iron bed between theirs, listening to their words and the clicking sounds of a contraband lighter, waiting to feel their cigarettes burn into my flesh.

Why was I there? I was there because it was a dumping ground for people who had nowhere else to go.

It had been the first semester of my junior year in college. I was enrolled in the University Honors Program and had successfully completed a prestigious summer internship. Still, I struggled constantly with suicidal thoughts—orders; I just couldn't get them out of my head. It happened several times a day, at all different times, even when I wasn't feeling particularly depressed.

Ever since I was a child, I had heard a suicidal voice. But in my late twenties, when I finally got to college, the voice became even more insistent. My energy was divided between doing my schoolwork, maintaining my work-study job, and keeping myself alive. I had to monitor myself minute by minute, talking myself out of acting on the suicidal thoughts.

I thought part of the problem might have been the medication I was on. During a short hospitalization in the psychiatric unit of a local hospital, I shared my concerns with my psychiatrist. He seemed appalled at my suggestion that the medication he had prescribed might be exacerbating the problem. Prozac was the miracle drug of the 1980s.

"It works for everyone else," he told me, emphasizing the word else.

I never found an effective way to respond to that statement. Oh, I had things to say—things like, but I'm not everyone else! I'm me! I don't know why these drugs aren't helping me—but they're not!

I wanted to tell him about how I felt so foreign, so alien from other people and their experiences that I was sure I couldn't be human. Of course, I knew telling him that—even though some parts of me often believed it to be true—would infuriate him and probably the entire staff, causing them to label me either borderline or schizophrenic, two labels I'd spent most of my life trying to shed. So, I didn't say anything. I was too ashamed. I just kept wondering why I was so different—so not-human. The psychiatrist's words echoed in my head. *It works for everyone else.* Even in the world of the mentally ill, I wasn't measuring up.

"But," I said, trying to find a voice that fit somewhere between pushy and pushover, "it's not working for me." I flashed back through the last thirteen years, to all of the psychiatrists and all of the drugs they tried on me, starting with Haldol, when I was sixteen years old. There was Desipramine, Stelazine, Elavil, Trilafon, Thorazine, Pamelor, BuSpar, Ativan, Valium, Xanax, MAO inhibitors, Tegretol . . . Tegretol, that one caused a near-fatal allergic reaction that put me in the ICU for almost two weeks; then the hospital sued me because I was only paying $25.00 every month toward my bill, instead of the $50.00 per month they demanded. No, the drugs didn't seem to help. They just made things worse.

Each new drug experiment brought its own set of symptoms. Some caused mood swings and behavior changes that scared me. Some became addicting. One, Compazine, put me into anaphylactic shock. Then there were the tardive dyskinesia-type symptoms—twitching lips, tongue flicking, hand tremors—brought on by the antipsychotic drugs.

"I'd like to try something else," the psychiatrist said, after I tried to plead my case against more experimentation. "Starting with your p.m. dose, I'd like to add lithium to the Prozac."

When you're in a situation where you have very little or no power, it's dangerous to stand up to the person or institution that does have power over you. I knew that. But I made the mistake of trusting that I was supposed to be assertive, confident, all the things written in the self-help literature and described in the handouts they gave us during psychoeducational groups.

"No more Prozac," I told him. "I think it's making things worse."

"Miss Fabio," he said, firmly. "You're not being very cooperative."

That's the last thing you want to be, when you're in a psych hospital—labeled "uncooperative." The only label worse than that is "borderline." Either one of them is bad news. If you were carrying around shame when you came in, being labeled uncooperative or borderline only adds to it.

The staff have their own way of dealing with "uncooperative" patients. Privileges are revoked, passes denied. They ostracize you, looking right past you, as if you're not even there. They only speak to you when absolutely necessary, and then, it's in quick quips. Orders.

Prozac and lithium—that's when the suicidal ideas became suicidal cravings. That's when it became almost impossible to come up with arguments against suicide. I call those years my suicide years—not because they're the only years that I ever thought about it; they're not—but because those are the years that I secretly tried to complete the task, and almost succeeded.

I remember waking up in the intensive care unit of the local hospital in Franklin Springs. A few days later, I was moved downstairs to the psychiatric unit. The psychiatrist assigned to my case realized the seriousness of my desires—that I had truly intended to end my life. He also believed that I was still suicidal.

He was right. Although I never said it, I honestly believed it was in everyone's best interest for me to succeed. I was thirty, depressed, plagued with violent flashbacks, in debt, had no family, and was living on grants, scholarships, and work-study funds. I took up space, and time, and money, yet seemed to serve no purpose.

He ordered me to remain in the hospital for ninety days. I tried to talk him out of that, because as far as I could tell, being hospitalized would only result in making things worse. I'd lose my job, my income, my apartment, yet I'd still be poor, depressed, and taking up space.

"I can't do that." I told him, "I'll lose my job. I won't have money for rent . . ."

"You can't worry about that now," he said, matter-of-factly.

"Breathing costs money," I told him, anxiously, trying to explain how each day of living requires money to maintain the body, how the debt accrues as the minutes pass. Once a month, the bills arrive, the debts portioned out in units of time—rent, gas, electric, heat, phone, medication. . . . Medication alone cost more than all of my other expenses put together.

"You need to be here," he told me. "You need to be in a safe place."

In the meantime, the hospital administration was busy processing my paperwork, adding up the expenses I'd already incurred in the emergency room, the intensive care unit, and the psychiatric unit. They submitted my bills to the student health insurance office, which, in turn, denied payment. According to the fine print in my student health insurance policy, injuries or illness related to suicide are not covered.

Patients without insurance are like a disease in the system; no one wants them, especially hospitals. The administration pressured the psychiatrist to discharge me. The psychiatrist, knowing he probably wasn't going to get paid, dropped my case. I found that out when a new doctor—a psychiatrist from the County Department of Mental Health—came to see me, informing me that I was now under his care.

In spite of pressure from the hospital administration, the county psychiatrist refused to discharge me. I guess he could tell that, although I wasn't talking about suicide, I still seemed depressed and hopeless enough to view it as a viable option. So he gave me a choice. Not a real choice, but about as close to a choice as you get, when you're a psych patient. I had the option of either being involuntarily committed to the state hospital in Linwood for ninety days, or of signing papers and voluntarily committing myself for ninety days. I didn't have the option not to go; I only had the option not to volunteer to go, in which case, they had the obligation to commit me.

The advantage of voluntarily committing myself, the doctor informed me, was that the staff at the state hospital would think I was cooperative. "You'll have an easier time of it, if you're cooperative," he advised. "You want to be compliant."

It didn't take long for me to discover that while I was waiting to be taken to the state hospital in Linwood, there wasn't much difference between the way I was treated and the way the involuntarily committed people were treated. We were all kept in the locked side of the psychiatric unit, which consisted of a narrow hallway; a room with a table, chairs, a television attached to the wall; and a row of sleeping rooms—small cells—each with a mattress on the floor and a video camera high on a corner of the wall.

Except for a few psychotic patients, no one talked to me. Staff people seldom came to that side of the unit; they just observed from the monitors at the nursing station.

Each day, my outlook became more and more hopeless. I started to become disoriented. It didn't matter what day or time it was—even though I got asked that every day, during the one or two minutes that the psychiatrist came to examine me.

Time scared me, mostly because I didn't know when it would happen. I knew that any minute, or hour, or day, my paperwork would complete its journey through the courts and then the sheriff's car would come for me. Two uniformed officers would handcuff me, lead me through the hospital hallways, into the elevators, down to the sheriff's car, through the town of Franklin Springs, and out onto

Highway 25 for the three-hour ride to Linwood. I'd seen it happen to other patients. I was waiting for it to happen to me.

Whenever I heard strange footsteps in the hallway—footsteps that didn't belong to the schizophrenic woman with the slow shuffling gait; footsteps that didn't belong to the adolescent boy who reeked of body odor—long quick steps that paced up and down the halls for hours at a time, I'd feel my heart stop. Panic would take over as I braced myself, wondering if it was them—the police, here to take me away. With each passing day, my depression became even more profound.

Time. I measured it in units of television programs. The blaring sound of game-show bells ringing, people clapping and cheering, and a man's voice exclaiming "Come on down!" marked a new day. The theme song from *M*A*S*H* meant the heavy metal hall door would open and a meal cart, filled with lunch trays, would roll down the hall until it reached a complete stop. If the *M*A*S*H* song played when it was dark, it meant that all of the lights would soon turn off and the television would finally become silent. It meant another day had passed.

I wasn't allowed to talk with higher functioning patients or to attend support groups or counseling sessions, because those things took place on the open side of the unit. My world was that long narrow hallway, and the few psychotic patients who came and went.

I spent most of my time trying to hypnotize myself into another place, or trying to fall into sleep. I lay on my mattress, hearing *The Price Is Right, I Love Lucy, Hogan's Heroes . . .* I started counting. The tiles on the ceiling, the dots on the tiles on the ceiling, how many verbs Bob Barker used. . . . I alphabetized and counted the syndicated television shows. That's how I put myself to sleep, listing programs in my head, tapping a different finger for each one. *Abbott and Costello, The Addams Family, Adam-12, Alfred Hitchcock Presents, All in the Family, Andy Griffith, Alias Smith and Jones, Alice, The Avengers, Ann Sothern, The A-Team, ALF . . .*

Occasionally, a dazed and confused, blond-haired patient wandered into my room. She was usually carrying something she had picked up in another room, trying to find just the right place to put the item down. Sometimes, she had a towel or a sock or a skirt on her head; sometimes she was completely naked.

Once, I told her that. "You're not wearing any clothes!" I cried incredulously, watching her walk slowly into my cell.

She stepped carefully, lightly, holding a book as if it were made of glass. For a moment, she stood in the corner studying the floor. Then she looked up at me, looked me right in the eye, a serious expression on her face. "Oh . . . it's okay," she assured me gently, pointing above her head, "I have my dress."

The psychiatrist came after every *Geraldo*. I didn't much like him—he never made eye contact, and really didn't seem interested in anything I had to say—but I still looked forward to his visits. He was a person. He didn't smell bad, and he wore clothes. Armani.

His social skills were lacking. He would sit in the plastic chair, staring out the window or down at his shoes. Cole Haan. I waited for him to begin. But he never did. Or perhaps he did, but his beginning was also his ending, because after about a minute, he'd sigh heavily and, as he rose from the chair, say, "Well, you don't seem any less depressed." Then he'd be gone, his footsteps becoming more and more faint until I'd hear the sound of a buzzer, and the slam of a door.

Eventually, my paperwork was complete, and I was moved to Linwood.

* * *

"I can go home?"

"Yes," the doctor said. "You don't belong here. You can go home as soon as your paperwork is processed. Unfortunately," he added, a worried look crossing his face, "it might take a couple of days."

"I can go home?" I repeated.

"You can go home."

"Thank you!" I said, rising from my chair and surprising myself by extending my hand. I was the scholar again. Confident. Self-assured.

He smiled and extended his hand. We stood there, psychiatrist and patient, shaking hands, as if we'd just completed a successful business deal.

"You can get better," he said. "Just not here. I'll do my best to push the paperwork through quickly," he added. "I'm worried about your safety."

I nodded and withdrew my hand.

Three days later, I climbed the gray wooden steps leading to my second-floor apartment, remembering the last time I'd been on those steps—carried, somehow, on something flat, faces staring down at me as I was wheeled across the sidewalk and slid neatly into an ambulance.

As I approached the landing and turned toward the door of apartment K3, I felt my heart thump once and then stop. Big, black, block letters stood defiantly, side by side, against a white background, spelling out the words NOTICE OF EVICTION.

There's nothing there, I told myself, turning away from the door. I took a deep breath, holding the crisp autumn air in my lungs, noticing, for the first time since I'd lived in that apartment, how pretty the parking lot was. The wind gently pushed golden-edged leaves off their branches, sprinkling some of them on cars, sport utility vehicles, and boats.

Canada geese honked, flying in an almost symmetrical formation, across a brilliantly blue sky. Two men and a woman—I could tell they were students—walking shorts, Hard Rock Cafe T-shirts, Birkenstock sandals, L.L. Bean backpacks slung across one shoulder—strolled across the lot, moving in a single unit, two walking, one slowly pedaling a mountain bike, all of them engaged in conversation.

I watched them, feeling envy. I was a student once, I heard myself whisper, a long time ago . . .

Actually, I had been a student during the first part of that exact semester. A junior. But I don't think I figured that out at the time. Time still confused me. It seemed like I'd been away for a year, but it had only been a little over a month. A few days in ICU, a week on the med/surg unit, two weeks in the psych unit in Franklin Springs, and then . . . a week in the state hospital. I shook my head again. Linwood.

I listened to the voices of the students crossing the lot, hearing snippets of conversation, laughter. I longed to be in school, to be a student, a regular person, with regular problems, like worrying about whether I'd get into the "right" sorority, or about what I'd wear to Homecoming; or about whether I should major in astrophysics or in modern dance. But those weren't my problems. Never were. I had bigger problems, like working up the nerve to get out of bed. I worried about someone finding out about my illness, about losing control of some part of myself, of acting on the suicidal feelings. I worried about getting sent to the hospital against my will. I worried about money, about becoming homeless.

I punched my hands into the pockets of my denim jacket and watched the students. My fingers felt something smooth, sharp, and metal. Quickly, I pulled my hand out of my pocket and stared, with amazement, at the objects. Keys! Sharps! The last thing they gave me, when I left Linwood, pushing them across the counter at me before the attendant unlocked the door and let me out. Keys! I stared at them. Unbelieving. Was I actually holding keys? I was. I could use them, go through doorways, start cars, unlock closets . . . without getting punished, or threatened with restraints.

A small manila tag was attached to the key ring with brown string. I looked at it, reading the letters scrawled across the dog-eared tag in black marker. F-A-B-I-O 69. I shivered, remembering Ward 69, where all patients whose last known address was in Mason County were kept. It didn't matter what your diagnosis was—antisocial personality disorder, manic-depression, schizophrenia, post-traumatic stress disorder, paraphernalia . . . if you were from Mason County, over age eighteen, and poor or without health insurance, you were "on 69."

I closed my eyes, shaking my head hard, trying not to see the movie playing in my head. Ward 69. I concentrated on grounding myself, focusing on the concrete things around me, trying desperately to orient myself to time and place—or at least to place. Stamping my foot lightly, I whispered, "floor."

"Trees," I added, forcing my eyes to widen. I focused on the parking lot. "Cars," I said softly, speaking as if I were reassuring a frightened child. "Yellow car. Blue car. Red pickup truck. Grey car. Bo—"

This is stupid! an adolescent commented.

I ignored the interruption and continued my efforts to distract each part of me from the movie—to bring them back onto the steps with me. "Boat," I continued. "Red car, blue car . . ."

But I was still there. Some part of me was still on Ward 69.

I pulled my left hand out of my pocket and reached for the gray wooden railing, touching it with the palm of my hand. "Porch," I whispered, feeling the warmth of the sun on the rough wooden surface. I know I felt relieved to be out of the hospital—to be free—but I also remember feeling scared, mostly because I wasn't used to doing things on my own, thinking about where I wanted to go, and then actually going there . . .

I inserted the key in the lock, the letters of the eviction notice staring hard at me. I listened for the click, and then was surprised when I heard it. Slowly, I pushed the door open. Perhaps, out of habit, I turned around, looking for someone with authority. It felt somehow wrong to pass through a doorway without permission, without someone's hand on my collar or tightly gripping my upper arm.

Cautiously, I stepped inside, turned, and softly pushed the door closed. Click. I stood still, my eyes taking in the sparsely furnished apartment. I don't know how long I stood there, a few inches from the front door, looking around the apartment. Remembering. I saw no signs of a fire, but there had been firemen in my apartment that night. Lots of them. Stomping around in heavy boots. Yelling at me in slow voices. A woman was trying to dress me. Someone was yelling my mother's name—Ms. Fabio, can you hear me?—shining a small, bright light into my eye. The ceiling loomed over their faces, as they worked on and around my body. I remember wondering if they could see me.

My eyes moved toward the tiny kitchen area. An open can of diet Crush was on the orange-stained counter. I had been sipping orange soda that night, flipping desperately through my address book, calling each of my friends, one at a time. I had been afraid—was losing control. The suicidal parts of myself were winning the argument. They pulled out bottles of prescription drugs, Ativan, Klonopin, trazodone, desipramine . . . I began calling for help, my fingers trembling as I dialed the phone numbers. I didn't know what I would say. It was so embarrassing, asking people to help me control myself. . . . Telephone answering machines, busy signals. . . . What happened after that . . . ?

I was afraid to move any further into the room, into the bedroom. The bathroom. I turned back around, pulled open the front door and jumped quickly out onto the porch, pulling the door hard behind me. But, once outside, I didn't know what to do there either. So I just stood there.

Eventually, I reached up and pulled the eviction notice down off the door, leaving the heavy staple intact. "I'll probably get billed for that too . . ." My voice sounded strange. It seemed like many days since I'd last spoken.

Being outside was as frightening as being inside—either place was too big, too open—I longed for a small room to hide in, some place safe where I wouldn't get lost. I rushed back into the apartment, slammed the door behind me, and leaned against it, arms outstretched, palms flat against the walls.

I spent most of those first days home moving from room to room, afraid to touch anything, unsure where to sit, where to stand, trying to ground myself, trying to get away from the movies and still-life photos flashing in my head, trying to erase the shame that had, during the last few weeks, wrapped itself even more tightly around me, in me, almost choking me. I'd sit on the edge of my bed, waiting for someone to tell me what to do, when to move, when to eat, when to go to bed. I knew no one was going to do that for me, but I just couldn't figure out how to do it for myself. I remember wanting to shower, to scrub off the stench of the hospital, the shame. But I couldn't seem to step into the tub. I just stood there, fully dressed, trying to figure out how to do it. Then, I would turn around and walk into the hall, where I would stand for a few minutes, or hours, and contemplate where to go next.

A few days later, seated at my kitchen table, I picked up the eviction notice and studied it. "I can't afford to live," I told myself.

Part of me opted for another try at suicide. Do it right this time, I heard myself demand. You need to be more careful, more accurate.

Part of me believed that my error was not in attempting to leave the Earth; it was in failing to succeed in the leaving. If you're failing at life, it's important that you succeed at suicide.

In a way, it made sense. I had discovered that if you try to leave and don't succeed, you're in an even more desperate place than you were before. You're still alone, still depressed and hopeless, still a burden on society—but you've lost what was left of your personhood. You're punished for trying to live and failing—and at the same time, for trying to die and failing.

No pills, an adolescent part joined in, too much time to change your mind . . . to much time for someone to notice . . .

I flashed back to the paramedics, the psych hospital, the commitment papers I was forced to sign.

The adolescent interrupted my thoughts: And forget starving; that takes way too long. Gives you too much time to change your mind.

It's gotta be quick . . .

We can't fail; that will land us back in the hospital.

Hospital? You mean jail, don't you?

I flashed back to Linwood. Some part of me was showing the rest of me a video. Ward 69.

"No," I heard myself, my adult self, say out loud. "We're not going back there."

I tried to think of ways to earn money, to get back into school, to get back my scholarships, to find an affordable place to live, to get back everything I'd lost.

A few days passed. The bills continued to arrive. Hospital bills, doctor bills, psychiatrist bills, ambulance bills, utility bills. Suicide became the only sensible option. I found myself vowing to do it right this time, to succeed, to use something that couldn't fail. I knew that in less than three days, the sheriff would accompany my landlord to my apartment, where he would stand guard while my landlord moved all of my possessions onto the curb. Suicide was the only sensible option. At least that's what most of me thought.

One stubborn part of me seemed to hang on though, struggled to search for a solution. That part of me gathered the rest of me around myself, like a mother gathering her children, and explained how we needed to try, how I needed their help . . . I asked them to trust me. Some of them did.

At about the same time, Betty, an older patient I had met during one of my hospitalizations on the local psych unit, came by to see how I was doing. When she saw me, she wrapped her heavy arms around me and pulled me close. I remember feeling safe; I wondered if that's what it felt like to be a daughter. Betty insisted that I come to live with her and her husband, Ted, in their mobile home up in the canyon, about fifteen miles from town.

At first I declined, mostly because I was sure that when she got to know me better she'd see me as a burden and resent my presence. She sat with me, on the edge of my bed, holding me, promising me everything would be okay. She would take care of me. Her husband wouldn't mind. We'd be like one big happy family.

We were. Sort of. But then one afternoon, a few weeks after I'd moved in with them, I found myself, once again, facing homelessness. While I was visiting Derrick, a patient I met during one of my hospitalizations, Betty telephoned me at his home and accused me of stealing her Prozac.

I experienced that familiar ground-crumbling-beneath-me feeling. My voice trembled. "What—what are you saying?" I stammered. "You're thinking that I took it?"

Silence.

I felt myself shift inside; my throat grew tighter, my voice rose. "I didn't! I didn't take your Prozac!" I cried. "I would never steal from you. From anybody! I never stole anything in my whole entire life!"

"Well," she said indignantly, "when I counted my pills today, there were some missing."

The adult part of me pushed forward. "I don't even use Prozac," I explained. "Remember? Prozac was a nightmare for me."

"All I know," she continued, "is that I count my pills every day. And today, there are three pills missing."

I became a child, begging to be heard, to be believed. "But it wasn't me," I pleaded, tears streaming down my face. "I don't know who took them," I begged. "Please, believe me—"

The phone line was dead.

About an hour later, Ted's truck arrived outside of Derrick's apartment. He dropped my suitcase and an open box of old books onto the driveway. Then he drove away.

Derrick and I stood there, on his driveway, looking at the suitcase, at the books. Neither of us said a word.

The Password to Larkspur Lane, I read silently, staring hard at the faded cover. I tried to enter the picture, to be Nancy Drew. I'm her, I told myself, staring hard at the strawberry blond-haired, blue-eyed detective.

Derrick's voice interrupted my fantasy. "You could stay here," he offered. "I have an extra bedroom. No strings."

I discovered, in the months after I'd moved into Derrick's house, that there were indeed strings. Actually, there were telephone cords and electrical appliance wires, guns, knives, bows, and arrows.

Shame hung over the table, like a cloud. And I breathed it in because, otherwise, I couldn't breathe at all. It was embarrassing, trying to explain to these women the route I'd traveled, the route that brought me to the safe house. I breathed in the smoke and coffee smell, and tried to speak. My voice sounded strange; detached.

"It was just supposed to be temporary," I explained, "living with him; it was just supposed to be till I could get back on my feet—get back everything I lost. . . . I got off all the meds," I said softly. "Found an apartment. Got back my scholarships. Everything was beginning to work out."

I looked up at the women's faces; some were blank, uninterested. Some nodded, encouraging me to continue. I wanted to tell them about how ever since I could remember I had longed for a safe place to call home. How when I began to believe such a place didn't exist on earth, I created it in my head. I wanted to be able to explain about how as my body grew, little pieces of myself seemed to chip off and become whole new parts of me—a six-year-old girl, two eight-year-old girls, a sad and thoughtful peer-rejected sixth-grader, an angry adolescent, a slightly self-absorbed bulimic beauty pageant contestant, a scholar. . . . I wanted them to understand that I'm not psychotic, or borderline, or schizophrenic—that I'm just somebody who has spent most of her life trying to figure out how to feel safe in a very unsafe world. I wanted to tell them how I had lost my personhood—how I'd become one of the homeless, the mentally ill. I wanted to tell them about the depression, about how one part of me could convince the rest of me that I had no value. I wanted to tell them all the things I'd been trying to say for so long—all the things I'd discovered it was not okay to say to a psychiatrist or psychologist. I wanted them to listen and believe me without simply labeling me and then discarding me. I wanted to show them the very me I was at that moment—all of me, and not be ashamed.

I wanted to, but I knew I couldn't. Not just because it wasn't the appropriate place for me to share all of that—but because some small part of me worried that if I let on about the internal voices, about the different parts of myself, these women would abandon me too. So I reached inside and tried to soothe and silence each part of me, gently pushing them to the back of myself. Then, I pushed an adult part of me forward; I think it was the scholar. And slowly, she began to speak.

The Waiting Room

Kathleen M. Kelley

While my mother's memory of her life
was being shocked from her,
shaken like cereal from a box
upstairs at the wiswall hospital,
i would wait downstairs for them to finish,
hiding behind the staircase,
a spiral that marked up,
line after line of hand-crafted spindles,
order on the polished oak floors, no
convulsions in the flowered parlor
or on the draperies that matched.

Something shocked also out of me,
my shamelessness,
though everyone was kind to me—nurse Louise
with her paper cups of water
and Alice at the switchboard, who showed me
where the bathroom was,
the nameless orderlies
who walked my mother down the aisle
like a bride on their arms,
helped her remember who had driven her
to the electroconvulsive shock treatment,
helped her remember her children, their names,
when it was all over.

Thereafter
I could always be counted on
to stop *myself* at the fence.
It would never become necessary
to cut *me* down to size
cut *me* off at the knees.

Home Sweet Nuthouse

Sara Kirschenbaum

The first night in the nuthouse was starkly sweet. We motley crew of patients lined up in our stocking feet and bathrobes at the medicine dispensary. Once we were handed our tiny paper cups holding colorful morsels of chemical hope, we headed back to our silent rooms. It was generously warm on the ward and no one needed much in the way of robes or covers. The lights were turned low but still offered enough illumination for the sleepless wandering that would keep our floor busy all night. My bare and simple room came as a relief. The empty walls left little for my obsessive thinking to work with.

As I tossed and turned in my little bed with the thin hospital-issue blanket, I noticed a nurse periodically tiptoeing into the room and peering at me. Shortly after her 3:00 a.m. tiptoe, I stood up and shuffled on the spotless shiny floor to the nurse's station to find out what these silent forays were all about. I had become used to watching hours grind by at night but I was not used to company. The nurse at the desk told me that when new patients come in, the nurses check on them hourly for at least the first twenty-four hours. I asked to see my chart and she turned her clipboard around so I could see the notations on my sleep and agitation levels. I was not alone with my misery; I had a witness. As I talked to the night nurse I heard how sane, coherent, and intelligent my voice sounded. For months I had heroically put on a lucid front. Now in the dim night light both my suffering *and* my stamina were revealed. I was going to like it here.

The dependable rules were a relief from the chaos and doom in my mind. It wasn't a locked unit, but you had to earn privileges, incrementally, to walk past the double doors, venture down the hall, get into the elevator, and step out into the cold fresh air of Massachusetts. It was a comfort not to be allowed out; it was about time someone reigned in my world. The psych ward felt safe, secure, and even cozy, like a small Club Med for troubled minds.

The trouble, it would be easy to say, was postpartum depression after the birth of my first baby, Sage. But in truth the pregnancy had been almost as bad as postpartum. My psychiatrist was a brilliant woman whose daily attention at the hospital was light therapy for perpetual darkness. She had discovered a hormonally triggered obsessive-compulsive disorder (OCD) and had, in the past two years, helped two dozen other new mothers with the disorder regain their lives. I was case study number 26. By the time I checked myself into the hospital, I was in a major depression in addition to the intrusive and sometimes violent thoughts from the OCD. I could not eat, sleep, hold my baby, or do anything of use. The night before I consented to go to the hospital, I was up all night on the phone, holding a full glass of milk in my hand that I couldn't bear to drink, listening to my best friend tell story after story to distract me from the knowledge that I was so sick with anxiety that I could hardly walk. At 6:30 in the morning I called my psychiatrist at home, in bed, waking up her husband, and then her, to say that I was ready to go in.

The morning that we left to take me to the hospital, I put my favorite purple and green paisley scarf curled inside Sage's cradle so that when he went to bed that night without me, my scent could hold him if not my arms. He was barely two months old.

The idea of being admitted had been both a solace and horror of last resort. Now I found myself on a get-acquainted tour of the thing I had feared. This place was real: the textured weave of the white cotton blanket on my bed; the polite, discouraged roommate; and the psych evaluations conducted by novice masters of social work students. One pimply-faced intern tested my anxiety index. When he got to the section on abstract thinking he asked me to interpret the phrase "a rolling stone gathers no moss." The best I could come up with was "as long as you keep moving you won't get in trouble," even though this rolling stone philosophy hadn't helped me much in the past eleven months.

After the psych evaluation came the medical workup. The hospital architects must have known that Misery and the Body were old friends; they had an examination room right in the psych ward. The hands of the nurses were soft and gentle as they moved me through the exam, looking for a physical source of my anguish. When they took my temperature they seemed surprised that it was 95 degrees Fahrenheit. Even my metabolism was unraveling. The negative temperature helped me believe that wellness had long ago escaped the reach of my willpower.

The first morning in the nuthouse came too soon. I was surprised that I had fallen asleep after my 3:00 a.m. rendezvous with the night nurse. Getting to the hospital had dragged me through the resistance of half a lifetime; now I had to get up for a daily rap group. I found it hard to navigate through the peppy schedule of check-in, therapy groups, and occupational therapy.

It *was* fun to check off the little boxes on the daily menus, assembling as many favorite things into each meal as possible: chocolate milk, corn muffin, lasagna, orange slices, kiwi slices, pickled beets, brownie, chocolate chip cookie. For some reason I didn't worry about wasting food; I'd check off as many boxes as I felt like and taste each thing.

At mealtime, a jury of anorexics hovered around as we all ate. They were tragic. Their caloric laser beams scanned each meal— their own and everybody else's: "Does it taste good? How much did you eat already? How big was it? Does it have a lot of grease?"

The patients were the true salve of the nuthouse. We had checked our pretense, along with our overcoats, at the door. One bathrobed patient might say to another: "Good morning, how are you?" and get the casual response: "I was up from three till five with a panic attack but I finally got back to sleep. I'm still a little wigged out. And you?" Honesty was one benefit of the swamp we were all slogging through.

If the patients were at the core of our psych ward village, the staff (not including the psychiatrists who gave the orders) were peripheral. One day we ganged up on two meek-eyed workers who were running a rap group; we asked them why everyone kept telling us, "Don't cry. It will be all right." After all, we reminded them, we were having a bit of a bad time.

Once a young Hispanic woman started screaming on the green vinyl couch in the lounge. She was the only other new mother on the ward and I felt some postpartum sisterhood with her. She had been committed to our clubhouse when she tried to jump out a window. Now her slender brown body was curled up in a fetal position, moaning and screaming. The sight of her acute misery distracted me from my own and I went to comfort her. I held her hand and listened to her moans. Other patients gathered around and tried to help her feel more comfortable with pillows and blankets. Then someone went to tell a staff person. Then the trouble began. A large female nurse entered the room but seemed more horrified by patients touching each other than by the moaning and screaming. We were firmly instructed not to touch each other and were shooed from the room. The crying mother was told to calm down. A full two days of moaning later, the young woman finally persuaded the staff to let her go to the emergency room, which was only nine flights down. The next day the staff informed us, only the tiniest bit sheepishly, that she had passed a kidney stone.

I wasn't intimidated by the staff of the psych ward. Their kindness and attention were useful to me. I loved having someone assigned to me at all hours in case I needed to talk. I knew that the treatment marching orders came from my psychiatrist. She had trained all the nurses and doctors in this hospital in how to care for the pregnancy-triggered OCD that she had diagnosed. On the first day of my hospitalization I asked her if I could reveal to the staff my violent thoughts about my baby. I was worried that they might try to take my baby from me. My doctor said that staff understood my disorder but that it was probably prudent not to tell the interns too much.

Each day my son and husband came to visit. In the beginning I found it hard to hold Sage. His little spirit was so eager and searching. At two months old he was lifting his head on that little neck and looking straight into the soul of whoever held him, with his fine gold hair standing straight up. His blameless eyes would catch and see into my pathetic ones. I couldn't stand to let him see me as I was, or to look away.

One morning Bud came to visit with an awful cold. He asked if I could take care of Sage while he found someplace to rest. I asked a nurse if Bud could nap on my bed while I watched my son. The nurse said it was fine but *I* wondered if I could manage. Before I'd come to the hospital I had not been able to hold the baby. Riddled with anxieties, I was sure my eyes were somehow damaging him forever. How would he be able to bond with other people if his own mother couldn't accept his gaze calmly? Could I take care of him, even if I was in the hospital?

Bud slept for four hours. Minute by minute I held my baby, propped him up on the couch, showed him off to staff and patients, willed myself to stay on track. Nurses scrutinized me, but they were also encouraging. "You're doing a great job with your son, Sara!" I wondered what they were writing in my chart. Secretly, I felt deeply liberated to have handed over my self-scrutiny to others.

The psych ward was comforting to me, with its steady company of those worse off than I, as well as those almost recovered. It was a relief to be in the middle of a bell curve. The drugs that my doctor hoped would work for me were kicking in. The obsessive thinking no longer had to be tackled and subdued minute by minute. There were now huge breaks—maybe ten minutes long—in my battle with obsessive fears and horrible thoughts. Each morning when I showered, I could measure the waning vigor of my OCD by watching how superstitious I was about turning the water off at just the right moment. Life was getting easier but was not yet completely free of fear and obsession.

After nine days I was ready to leave but the discharge nurse was concerned. I had planned to return to work immediately, where I was responsible for over 200 employees. She wondered if I wanted to come back at night to sleep at the hospital. I secretly appreciated the offer. But when the next day came I walked out holding my tiny son and didn't turn back: through the double doors, down the hall, to the elevator, and into the bracing Massachusetts cold. My stride was big and palatably free. I didn't turn back, until just now, as I write my story.

Tonight I miss it, even though my life is better than I could have dreamed. Sage is a tall, handsome, happy eight-year-old and he has a feisty five-year-old sister. But tonight I want the monklike retreat from obligations, and the honest, casual intimacy with other patients. I want someone assigned to me at all times in case I feel like talking. I want to sleep in that silent, warm, awake ward with someone tiptoeing in each hour. I want a reunion so that I can eat dinner and check up on the anorexics. I'd like to celebrate our perseverance together with copious desserts, then all take our antianxiety pills before snuggling up for a big sleep over party in the TV lounge. After all, everyone needs a break once in a while.

i remember

Hadiyah Carlyle

i remember
being called into the principal's office
with the school psychologist
i remember
telling

saying on paper
what happened in the early mornings
at my house
on 1500 Munn Ave.
i remember
being told i was lying
and never to write again

i remember
resisting writing
standing naked
before school authorities
i remember
wanting to write a poem
wanting to shout out
but the words came down on me

i remember
all the devices
to make me forget
i remember
stretched out on the table
counting 10-9-8-
held down
one aide on each side

I remember
screaming
no no no
i remember
please god
hear me

i remember
it didn't take
i remember
the doctor called in
i remember
the orderly voice
she won't go out
i remember
an order
increase the voltage
i remember
passing out
to the shocks
electrical shocks

i remember
the fancy mental hospital
menopausal women
given shock treatments to forget
i remember
my innocence lost
to my father on top
i remember
a lot i shouldn't remember
the lonely nights
staring out the window on Munn Ave.
to the tree lined street

i remember
the cold winter days
climbing to the top
on Alaska king crab boats
working with my hands

in Bellingham
i remember
looking down
the chill
going through me
again and again
i remember my body
on cold hard mornings
frozen to the despair
of a woman coming to life.

Bathing in the Bin

Jo Patti

Unconsciously a libation,
she poured water over her shoulders
while sitting in a porcelain tub.
Nurses knelt beside her,
an orderly held a clipboard,
bright lights shot through her,
she was illuminated for their benefit—
every mark, every scar, every unusual feature
noted meticulously by men with pens.
Couldn't they wait?

Was she to be some fish bait
dangled on a hook for bigger prey,
attractive as long as she was squirming,
flapping as she was cast out,
her agonies as a lure to reel others in?
She splashed the water with her flipper feet,
eyes crawling all over her,
big men, white and black, gaped—
she was naked.

Couldn't they finish?
An undercurrent of voices
chanting possible medications,
Thorazine, Stelazine, Haldol,
Librium, Lithium, Zoloft.
She is never consulted,
but keeps laughing absurdly
as they roll her over,
stabbing her back with stares,
poking her with callous fingertips,

the water getting tepid,
her flesh rising from the chill.

They tell her not to wash her hair.
She stands robot-like waiting for towels.
Her flank is pinched before she receives them.
She keeps smiling to the end.
No one seems to get the joke.

Outtakes

Elayne Clift

Snakepit Sundays

Once a week I steel myself for the longest journey of my life: At the age of ten, I travel regularly to madness. My mother is in that most terrifying of places, a psychiatric hospital, and I cannot bear to let my father face it alone. We drive for an hour together, without speaking, each of us with our private vision of the hell awaiting us. At the entrance to the drab and foreboding institution where my mother has spent the last weeks in depressed silence among multitudes of demons, my stomach tightens. At the sight of my mother, once so elegant and beautiful, shuffling toward us in mismatched polyester, it nearly spills. Who is this woman looking so frightened and forlorn? How shall I rescue her? In the lounge, where plastic chairs line the walls as if to forbid any human discourse and the TV babbles incoherently, my mother says, "You've got to take me out of here. I can't stand it any longer!" I look at my helpless father, imploring him with my eyes, but he averts his. The doctors have said she needs to be here, where they can put electrodes to her brain to shock her into sanity and compliance. We take a walk to the canteen (my mother has ground privileges) where lucky inmates can smoke, drink Coke, and pretend that life isn't so bad after all. We tell my sad, angry mother that she will be home soon, that this is for the best, that we love her. She glares at us and a big, ugly laugh escapes her throat. "I don't belong here with these people," she says. "If I stay here I'll go crazy." Some people treat her as if she is crazy already. Or a naughty child. "Now, Reba," they say, "take your medicine like a good girl." When we leave, I feel my heart will break at the sight of her, abandoned. On the way out of the locked corridor, a woman with greasy hair slinks along the wall, touching it as if it is a lifeline. Another shouts to her husband, "Goddamn you to hell! You put me here!" The nurse clinks her keys. My mother disappears into the dungeon of the demented to suffer her torment in solitude for another week. Even at the age of ten, I know that where she is, and what is happening to her, is awful, and that she is powerless to stop herself as she slides down that slippery slope on her descent to Hell.

Keeping the Vigil

I stay home from school and when my mother is too long in the bathroom I knock and ask if she is okay. She is on unofficial suicide watch because she has said, "I'll kill myself if they try to take me back there! I won't have that torture!" That is what she calls it, never shock treatments, torture. The burn marks on her temples, not knowing it's my birthday, her other lapses, make me think she is right. She remembers, she says, being dragged bodily and against her will into the treatment room, the tongue depressor being shoved into her mouth, the restraints, the electrodes put to her head, the condescending nurses, the authority of the doctors who infantilize her into obedience. She even remembers the initial jolt. "I won't go back!" she sneers, her once beautiful black eyes glaring at me as if I am part of the conspiracy trying to destroy her. Her tongue lashes involuntarily out of her mouth; drug-induced tardive dyskinesia has made my mother snakelike. Just as her refusals of ECT have been judged pathological, so too have the untoward side effects she suffers from psychotropic drugs with which the experts experiment. The more she symptoms, the more they force into and upon her. (After all, "involutional melancholia," the curse of menopause, must be dealt with in the 1950s.) So when my mother shouts at me with controlled hysteria, "I'm not going back there!" I know it is the voice, not of a madwoman, but of someone utterly sane and desperate. It is the fight-or-flight response of a woman struggling for breath before sinking forever into the deep, dark sea.

Backwarded

It is long after the snakepit years. My father is dead. My mother has been in a chronic care facility, with time out when she can cope, because she can no longer care for herself during depressive episodes. (She is now diagnosed as bipolar, manic-depression having gone out with the 1960s). Once, when she has a particularly bad episode, her doctor, a small-town guy with a big-city ego, hospitalizes her, over-doses her on Mellaril, and leaves her on a back ward to die. She is, in his opinion, a hopeless geriatric. When I arrive to rescue her, she is contracted into a fetal position, her hair wild, her toenails uncut and beginning to curl over the tips of her toes. She is catatonic. I bundle her into the car for the long trip home, quivering with rage and fear. Months later, when she is recovered and volunteering for a senior citizen program, I call the creep who nearly killed my mother, and when he finally returns the call I put the question to him: How could you? (The lawyers have advised against a malpractice suit. It would only be won, they say, if my mother had not recovered.) He does not wish to discuss the case, he says. Then, he sends me a bill for the telephone call.

A Long Thirty Years

The time has come for my mother to have custodial care. She wants very much to live near me at the Hebrew Home for the Aged. I arrange the psychiatric intake, required because of her history. I take half a day off from work and drive across town, arriving fifteen minutes early for our 3 o'clock appointment. At 3:45 the psychiatrist arrives. He explains nothing, makes no apology for his tardiness. I register my distress. He says, "You seem to have a problem with psychiatrists." I respond, "Let's just say it's been a long thirty years." Three weeks later, my mother is refused admission to the Hebrew Home. Every year when they call me for an annual contribution because of "the loving care we provide our Jewish elderly," I say "Tell it to my mother."

Courtesy Transfer

I am nineteen, a student, and profoundly depressed. I seek help. At the student health center I am referred to Dr. C., on-campus consultant. Dr. C. is a dour version of Oscar Levant, dark haired, brooding, unsmiling, without affect (that, he implies, is my job). After several sessions I feel no relief. His demeanor, I tell my roommate, is enough to depress Will Rogers. I ask him why he never smiles, never says hello to me in the dining hall. "I am not your boyfriend," he says. "Perhaps you are confusing your feelings for me." (Is this guy crazy?) "It's just fundamental courtesy," I say. "I am not ashamed to be here."

He glares at me like I have carelessly dropped my brain somewhere and he will be charged with finding it. I wander out of the session astounded. I never go back. I am unwilling to trust my psyche to someone who can't even acknowledge that I exist.

The Power Sparrow

My friend has entered the hospital for stomach pain. When they can't diagnose its source, she is admitted to the psych ward "for a few days rest." Ten weeks, several drugs, copious recreational therapy sessions, and one shrink later, she is discharged to a day care center where she continues to make mosaic ashtrays while her psychiatrist discusses her case with her passive-aggressive husband. Many years later, degree, career, and divorce papers in hand, she runs into the doctor who worked so diligently to convince her that she had serious pathology to deal with. He does not remember her. But she remembers him, and his allegations of sexual dysfunction, his labels and laments about her unrealistic expectations, his treatment regimes designed to make her conform. Then, she wonders how this little sparrow of a man, this diminutive, disheveled guy who seems so intimidated by her strength and sound persona, could have had so much power over her during those terrifying days when he didn't seem to see her or hear her pain. She can laugh now at the thought of this wimpy little man playing with her mind. But she didn't laugh then, in the days when women cowered and men controlled. Then, she listened, and tried very hard to be a good girl. It took her years to find her way back from a time of tyranny when sparrows ruled the world.

You, Doctor Martin

Anne Sexton

You, Doctor Martin, walk
from breakfast to madness. Late August,
I speed through the antiseptic tunnel
where the moving dead still talk
of pushing their bones against the thrust
of cure. And I am queen of this summer hotel
or the laughing bee on a stalk

of death. We stand in broken
lines and wait while they unlock
the door and count us at the frozen gates
of dinner. The shibboleth is spoken
and we move to gravy in our smock
of smiles. We chew in rows, our plates
scratch and whine like chalk

in school. There are no knives
for cutting your throat. I make
moccasins all morning. At first my hands
kept empty, unraveled for the lives
they used to work. Now I learn to take
them back, each angry finger that demands
I mend what another will break

tomorrow. Of course, I love you;
you lean above the plastic sky,
god of our block, prince of all the foxes.
The breaking crowns are new
that Jack wore. Your third eye
moves among us and lights the separate boxes
where we sleep or cry.

What large children we are
here. All over I grow most tall
in the best ward. Your business is people,
you call at the madhouse, an oracular
eye in our nest. Out in the hall
the intercom pages you. You twist in the pull
of the foxy children who fall

like floods of life in frost.
And we are magic talking to itself,
noisy and alone. I am queen of all my sins
forgotten. Am I still lost?
Once I was beautiful. Now I am myself,
counting this row and that row of moccasins
waiting on the silent shelf.

II: THERAPY

From *Welcome to My Country*

Lauren Slater

"So who wants to take the case?" asks Dr. Siley, the director of both the inpatient and outpatient facilities where I work. He folds the initial intake evaluation from which he's been reading back into its green file.

None of the other clinicians offer. A woman as outrageously demanding and consistently suicidal as this one is would add a lot of pressure to anyone's job. Ellen looks away. Veronica busies herself with the pleats on her skirt. The staff room stays quiet.

"What about you?" Dr. Siley says, looking in my direction. He knows my numbers are down. My job description states I'm responsible for seeing at least twenty in his outpatient clinic, in addition to the chronic schizophrenics in his residential program.

"Well," I say, "she sounds like a lot of work."

"Who isn't?" Veronica says.

"Why don't you take her, then?" I say.

"I'm full," Veronica says.

"And you aren't," Dr. Siley adds, pushing the file across the table toward me.

The phone rings six, maybe seven times, and then I hear a tiny voice on the other end—"Hello," it whispers, and I announce myself, the new therapist, let's make an appointment, look forward to meeting you, here's where the clinic is, in case you forgot—

"Can't," the voice weeps. "Can't, can't." I hear the sound of choking, the rustle of plastic. "Ten times a day," the voice says. "Into thirty-three-gallon bags. I've spent"—and sobbing breaks out over the line—"I've spent every last penny on frozen pizzas. There's blood coming up now."

"You need to be in a hospital, then," I say.

"Oh, please," the voice cries. "Put me in a hospital before I kill myself. I'm afraid I'm going to kill myself."

I tell her to sit tight, hang on, and then I replace the receiver. I know the routine by heart. I call 911, give the ambulance company her name and address, tell them there's no need to commit her because she said she'd go willingly. Next they'll take her to an emergency room, and after that she'll be placed on an inpatient unit somewhere in the state. She can't come into our own program's inpatient unit because she's neither schizophrenic nor male, the two criteria for admission. She'll stay wherever she is put anywhere from three days to four weeks, enough time, probably, for her to forget I ever called, to forget she ever wandered into the clinic where I work. At the hospital they'll likely set her up with an aftercare psychologist affiliated with their own institution, and he or she will have to deal with what sounds like her enormous neediness. And I, lucky I, will be off the case. Or so I think.

Two days later a call comes through to my office. "Ms. Linda Cogswell tells us you're her outpatient therapist. Could you come in for a team meeting next Monday afternoon?"

"Well, I don't even know her, actually. I was assigned the case, but before I could meet her she had to be hospitalized. Where is she?"

"Mount Vernon. I'm her attending psychologist here. Would you be willing to meet with us regarding her aftercare plans?"

Mount Vernon, Mount Vernon. And suddenly, even though it's been years, I see the place perfectly all over again, the brick buildings, the green ivy swarming the windows. The nurses who floated down the halls like flocks of seagulls, carrying needles in their beaks. My heart quickens; a screw tightens in my throat.

"Mount Vernon?" I say. Of all the hundreds of hospitals in Massachusetts, why did it have to be *this* one? And another part of me thinks I should have been prepared, for eventually past meets present; ghosts slither through all sealed spaces.

"Look, I don't know the woman at all," I repeat, and I hear something desperate in my voice. I try to tamp it down, assume a professional pose. "I mean, the patient, although technically assigned to me, has not begun a formal course of psychotherapy under my care."

A pause on the line. "But *technically,*" the voice retorts, "she is under your care, yes? You have some sort of record on her? Your clinic agreed to take the case?"

"Yes," I say. "Well . . . yes."

"Next Monday, then, one o'clock, North—"

"Two," I interrupt bitterly. "North Two."

"Good," she says. "We'll see you then."

The Caregivers' Dance

Catherine Spensley

Doctors

One day my sister announces that she is going to marry one of the most famous men in the world. It's during a period when she keeps checking herself into the Seventh-Day Adventist hospital in her neighborhood because she thinks her heart has stopped beating. She also suspects her brain of hemorrhaging, but believes the leakage is too small for the doctors to detect.

My sister, well into her forties, has never acted this strangely before. I carry around my concern for her constantly, a problem demanding a solution, but I don't know what I can do. Living on the opposite coast from her, I telephone often and remain hopeful that whatever stress she's undergoing will pass.

After a few months my sister's complaints of physical ailments subside, but she continues to mention the wedding, which she insists is imminent. I remember saving a newspaper article about a doctor specializing in erotomania, the pathological pursuit of love. I decide to contact the doctor. He immediately sounds interested.

"Looks like your sister is a classic case," he says. "May I ask you some questions?"

"Okay."

I'm excited to have found a doctor who will tell me what's happening with my sister. I answer his probing questions about her and about me and about the rest of our family, but when I ask him for specific advice regarding my sister, he's less generous with his enthusiasm. A matter of trying different drugs, he remarks quickly. Hit or miss. No real cure. No one understands the biology of the disease.

"But I'd like to include you in my research. May I send you my questionnaire?"

"Okay," I say, but I never receive his questionnaire.

A month later my sister checks into a nearby Catholic hospital, after the Seventh-Day Adventists tell her their beds are full. I wonder how this new hospital will know about her other hospitalizations, and I worry that they won't have enough information to make an accurate assessment. As much as I respect my sister's sovereignty over her own affairs, given her impaired condition, I decide that she needs a family advocate.

For the next several days I try to get in touch with the psychiatrist assigned to her case, but keep getting his voice mail. On the fourth day I call the nurse's station on my sister's ward, and a nurse warns me that some doctors are reluctant to speak about their patients over the phone. I'm troubled that my sister's doctor might fall into this category.

A few days later the doctor calls me at work, collect. I tell him I'll call him right back. When I call him right back, I get his voice mail. Later in the day I finally reach him on the phone.

"Listen," he says, "I've received plenty of messages about what you seem to want."

I'm surprised by his patronizing tone, even though the nurse had tried to prepare me, I realize. My messages had informed him of my sister's recent pattern of checking herself into hospitals and had requested an opportunity to speak with him regarding his ideas for diagnosis and treatment—none which I consider unusual, let alone bothersome.

"So Doctor, what do you think should be done?"

"Why are you asking me that? You seem to have it figured out."

We've obviously gotten started off on the wrong foot and he's the type to hold a grudge; still, I'll never understand why some doctors feel they have a professional right to be rude.

"Okay," I say calmly, not wanting to further prejudice my sister's case, "aside from what I want, as her doctor what do you think is the best course of treatment?"

"Outpatient treatment."

"But my sister doesn't think she has a mental problem, does she?"

"No, she still thinks she has something wrong with her physically."

"Then how can we expect her to seek treatment on an outpatient basis?"

"That's what happens in these cases," he replies sharply. "Now, if there's nothing else . . ."

I can no longer hide my frustration. "I'm sorry, doctor, but I'm not sure this is very helpful."

"Well, that's your opinion," he says, and he hangs up.

Mental Hospitals

My sister ends up in a state mental hospital, although I'm not exactly sure how this happens. My concern now is that she'll become a number in a large institution. When I speak to the social worker about my sister seeing a psychologist, she confirms my fears about the system being overcrowded. She says doctors must choose among the patients they believe individual therapy will benefit the most, but she thinks my sister is a good candidate. I'm relieved that this social worker seems ready to go to bat for my sister, and I'm optimistic about a breakthrough during this stay. Also, the hospital has a toll-free phone line, which will save me lots of money. I'm impressed.

I check in with the social worker once a week, and after three weeks she informs me that my sister will probably remain in the hospital for a while because they feel they can do her some good. She declines to be more specific, but this news feels like progress, and I'm comforted.

I continue calling the social worker regularly, but she's started to sound discouraged. I've detected traces of apathy in her voice before and thought it was social-worker burnout, but now that my sister has been in the hospital for over two months, I'm beginning to think I can't blame her. In fact, I'm tired of talking to doctors and social workers. And I have no idea if it's doing any good.

I call the hospital when I get back from vacation and learn that my sister is doing much worse, that she is refusing to take any medication and has gone into a psychotic state. At the moment she is pacing the halls and is afraid to eat anything.

It's Wednesday, and I leave a message to speak with the doctor. On Friday I leave another message. On Monday, finally, I reach him on the phone. I ask him what's happened.

"What's happened," he says, "is that the courts have taken away the institution's right to force medication."

He goes into greater detail about the issue than I need to hear right then. When he pauses, I steer the conversation back to my sister.

"Do you think she can be talked into taking her medication?"

"You have two options," he barks. "You wait until she deteriorates to a point where she's harmful to herself or to others and then the institution can force her to take medication, or you have a family member assigned as medical guardian, which is much easier to do."

I ask several other questions about my sister's fear of the medications, but the doctor ignores them, merely restating the two options.

"I don't understand why you keep repeating those two options," I say. "I understand them, but I want to know . . ."

"Look," he snaps. "Any psychological considerations are irrelevant. I'm unable to do anything for her in this state." He repeats the two options.

"How does someone become a medical guardian?" I ask.

"Go to a lawyer."

"What kind of medication would you put her on?"

"What?" he says, openly angry now. "You should know what medication she's supposed to be on. She's your sister. And you're the one who told me," he adds.

He's referring to an earlier conversation when I informed him that a certain drug had worked well for other family members.

"And off the top of my head," he says, "I don't know what medication she's on. You should be taking notes or something."

Later I wished I'd defended myself, saying my sister's medication had been switched so often that I'd lost track of the changes, but his hostile tone had succeeded in intimidating me.

"Sorry, I can no longer speak to you," he tells me.

"Goodbye, sir," I reply, finding some satisfaction in knowing I'd kept my cool better than he had.

I talk to the social worker and she confirms that the hospital can't do anything until my sister agrees to take medication, and she advises me to call the public health department to find out about legal guardianship. She cannot comment about the doctor's response to me, she says, since she wasn't present, but she doesn't understand why he neglected to mention that he'll need to do a complete medical workup on my sister to see what kinds of medication she can now tolerate.

I feel like writing to the doctor to vindicate myself, but I'm afraid of repercussions to my sister's care. My better judgment tells me to let it go and follow the advice of the social worker by looking into medical guardianship. I make about fifteen calls to various state and county mental health departments, but no one seems to know anything about it. I wait for several people to call me back, but who knows if they will?

My Sister

I call the hospital to see if my sister has eaten anything and learn that her weight has dropped to eighty-five pounds and that she's been moved to a medical ward. I reach the social worker on the new ward, who is a man and sounds young. He tells me he doesn't know if my sister is eating or not, because she won't be offered any food until 5:30, when dinner is served.

"Given the circumstances," I say, "don't you think you could offer her some food now?"

"We've been offering her things to drink," he says, "which is really more important."

"How about a milk shake?" I suggest. "She really loves ice cream."

"We don't have ice cream, but we have Sustacal, which is a high-nutrient drink."

"Okay, can you offer her that?"

"I'll remind the staff," he says.

"And can you remind my sister that she's promised me to eat?"

He says that he will, but something in his voice, a mixture of distraction, perhaps skepticism, leads me to think that he'll forget.

Later that afternoon I call the hospital and the nurse passes me to the somatic doctor on the ward, who tells me she wants to force-feed my sister with tubes through her nose. It's safer than IV, she says, less risk of infection.

I feel panic and realize I don't completely trust doctors. I tell her I want to speak with my sister once more. I ask the doctor if she will offer my sister a Sustacal while I'm speaking to her. The doctor agrees.

My sister comes to the phone and all she says is, "I'm sorry," several times, sounding extremely weak. The rest of the time she continues to breathe into the phone, but doesn't say anything. I have the feeling she's thought she could commit suicide this way. After a few minutes the doctor comes back on the phone and says they will hook her up.

Me

I decide I need to go to the hospital immediately. The next day I fly across the country and drive two more hours to get out of the city and into the cornfields. The state mental facility was built in an era when it was culturally acceptable to apply the *out of sight, out of mind* axiom to the mentally ill. I am struck, however, by the beauty of the sprawling campus: the old, hardwood trees; the lush green lawns; the calm and quiet—no one seems to be around. The century-old brick buildings are widely dispersed, and the medical building has a large covered porch, where I picture sitting with a cool drink, watching a game of croquet on the groomed lawns below—although this diversion vanishes as soon as I step inside the lobby with its scuffed, institutional-green walls and freight-sized elevator open and waiting to take me up to the ward.

On the third floor I stand outside a locked door for several long minutes, until a nurse sees me waving through the glass and ambles her way down the long hallway to let me in. I am shown to my sister's room, which she shares with three other women, all elderly, and one of whom keeps screaming. I'm shocked by my sister's appearance. She is thinner than I could have imagined. Her hair is matted and tied in knots. Her face is ashen. She is curled up in a fetal position. A nurse is sitting on the end of her bed, watching TV. I gently shake her. She wakes up. She smiles. I can tell she is glad to see me, and she nods when I ask if she remembered I was coming. I try to hold onto this fact as encouraging.

The next day as soon as I'm let into the locked ward her internist, an Indian woman, rushes up to me.

"Can't you get her out of here? Can't you take her back to California with you? It's such a waste, a smart girl like that."

"I-I don't know," I stammer. "I'm not sure California is any better."

Later when I'm talking to my sister's psychiatrist, he brushes off these comments. He agrees that relocation is not the issue at hand, but still, the woman has upset me.

I'm pleased with this new psychiatrist, a retired military doctor. He is warm and friendly and immediately puts my mind at ease. He explains the medication plan that he believes will work best for my sister, and he says she'll be started on it as soon as they receive the legal authority to proceed. He assures me that my sister's case is quite controllable with drugs, and I feel profound relief that at last my sister has arrived under the care of a doctor who has compassion and seems confident that she will recover. And yet within moments, this doctor informs me that he'll be retiring the next day.

I locate the social worker and he's more or less what I expected: young and inexperienced, but at least he seems enthusiastic, for which I am grateful. During my visits I grow to like him, even though I think he lacks sensitivity. At one point I ask him what he thinks my sister might like for her birthday, which is the following day, and he says he doesn't know but he'll think about it. Later, when I'm in the lounge with my sister, he comes barging in. "I don't know if I'm bursting any surprises," he says to my sister, "but what would you like for your birthday?"

My sister ignores the question and him.

I remind the nurses about my sister's birthday, and I tell them that she has agreed to get a haircut. I explain how I think this will help her self-esteem, and they say they will call the beauty parlor to see if anyone can be sent to the ward the next day to cut her hair. When I arrive at the hospital in the morning, I check with the nurses and they tell me that they haven't been able to get through to the beauty parlor, but will try again. I let the social worker in on my plan and he thinks it's a great idea. He reassures me that he will check up on the staff's progress.

I hear nothing all morning, so around noon I ask the nurses about it and they report that they still haven't gotten through. Finally in the middle of the afternoon a nurse finds me and says, "The beauty parlor won't be able to give her an appointment for three weeks. They'll cut her hair, but they won't wash it or anything else."

"Okay," I say, stunned, but continuing to scheme. "Surely there's someone on this ward who cuts hair."

She tells me about a nurse who gives haircuts to some of the staff and that she comes on duty at three. I'm excited about this new solution, but shortly after three o'clock, this particular nurse comes to me and claims that she can't legally cut my sister's hair because she isn't licensed.

"Fine," I say. "May I cut her hair?"

The nurse thinks for a second. "Sure, you can do anything you want."

She gets me a pair of scissors and, although I have no experience in cutting hair, within minutes the mats are finally removed from my sister's hair.

Before I leave to go back to California, my sister and I meet with her newest doctor, although he tells us that he's only filling in for the next month until they can find someone else. The doctor asks my sister if she thinks she's too fat and that's the reason she doesn't want to eat. My sister doesn't reply, and he doesn't seem to care. On our way out of the office, I ask for an opportunity to speak with him alone before I leave the hospital, but when I try to find him later, no one knows where he is. The nurse tells me they have no way to reach him since he doesn't carry a beeper.

The social worker suggests I check up regularly on the clinical review panel, who will decide if my sister is a harm to herself or others and can be forced to take medication. Keep up the pressure, he says. It really helps.

It's been a difficult trip, but I'm glad I've come because I feel that I've done some good. My sister responded to me, and I can tell that the nurses and social workers were impressed with the small amount of progress—especially when my sister and I were playing duets on the piano. I have arranged for her to have private sessions with the music therapist.

Weeks go by with no real change. Then the social worker calls and informs me that since my sister is in the hospital under voluntary status, the clinical review panel has no jurisdiction and we must go the route of medical guardianship. I let him know that when I called the hospital's legal department to check on the progress of the guardianship papers, they had said that they'd removed the medication statement from the documents, because they thought the clinical review panel was taking care of that. The social worker says he'll look into it. Later he calls me back and says I need to send another official letter requesting guardianship. I have already sent many letters at this point, but of course I will keep doing so.

I send letters to the superintendent of the hospital requesting expedience in my sister's case. I send letters to the staff attorneys clarifying the medication statement. I copy all her doctors and all her social workers, on all the various wards she's been on.

I realize now that I am playing the dance, and will continue to play the dance, with as many mental health professionals as I have to, because this is something I am able to do.

The social worker calls to inform me that the doctor has neglected to put the medication statement on the guardianship papers and that he is going to have to track down the doctor and have this corrected—yet I barely hear what the man is saying, because he's also told me that my sister has started eating. I ask to speak with her.

I can tell from the sound of my sister's voice that she's turned the corner. She says she's sorry for having caused me so much trouble. And she tells me that she's been playing duets on the piano with her music therapist. He has photocopied some sheet music for her, and she is going to practice over the weekend.

The Psychoanalyst's Daughter: A Memoir

Karen Wunsch

Like the minister's wanton child, I wasn't a very good analysand.
Instead of freely associating, I tended to whine about any little thing
that happened to be bothering me. Of course even topics like the frus-
trations of returning clothes to Bloomingdale's could have been rich
material, if I'd been able to explore them in depth. Periodically, duti-
fully, I'd bring up the various separations from one or both of my parents during what I called my "famous traumatic childhood"—but the
stories came to feel dry and mechanical even to me. I'd also repressed
many childhood memories, but rather than fight the good fight with
my unconscious, I tended to just change the subject. And resisted analyzing my resistance.

My analyst was a generation younger than my father, but like him,
a fairly traditional Freudian. Trying to conduct a more or less "classi-
cal" analysis, he tended to be nondirective. When he'd occasionally
break his silence to push me to explore my unconscious more deeply, I
tended to clam up as if I were a criminal and he the FBI—an analogy
I doubtless censored. Following theory, he'd say little.

When I wasn't complaining about life's ups and downs, I'd say little, too.

Even when I'd bring up something more relevant to me at the time,
like problems I was having teaching college English, I tended to hold
myself at arm's length. Periodically I'd mutter something like, "I hate
feeling obligated to charm my students"—trying to speak about myself and charm in the same breath, a juxtaposition I sensed it must be
difficult for my analyst to make. No comment.

My analyst's Upper East Side office was in one-half of a brown-
stone, and he lived on the other side with his wife and several small

children, whom I occasionally saw and/or heard. My fantasies about his personal life could have made rich material for us to explore, but another irony I wasn't interested in pursuing was that although I was coming to see that my father's separation of his professional and private lives was too rigid, I (secretly) resented the extent to which my analyst's two lives intersected. (Secretly) upset that he wasn't the blank screen (for his patients to project upon) that my father had so dogmatically, I now saw, tried to be, rather than analyze these feelings I did my best to ignore them.

Occasionally our silence would be shattered by loud shrieks and thumpings.

"Yes?" my analyst might prompt as I'd try to ignore something like a child screaming, "You're a big fat poopie."

These conflations of his professional and personal lives must have reminded me of times I'd overhear my father dictating notes about his patients, or of the times in his waiting room I'd fantasize about seeing a patient or occasionally even see one. I did my best to censor these associations. I'd be lying on the couch, periodically trying to tug down my fashionable miniskirt—this was the mid-1960s.

"Yes?" my analyst might say tentatively, the analytic version of "A penny for your thoughts." He'd be sitting in a chair positioned behind my head, presumably all ears.

Silence.

Occasionally I'd hold out some withered flower from the sparse bouquet of my childhood memories. I (secretly) saw him dashing next door as soon as I left, to tell his wife that he couldn't take much more . . .

Another problem (and, given my father's rigid adherence to Freudian dogma, an additional irony) was that despite analytic theory that stipulates that the patient's significant financial sacrifice for therapy should goad him or her to terminate sooner rather than later—because when I started treatment I wasn't working—my father paid. Even when I began teaching and—although I didn't earn enough for a "classic" analysis—could have contributed something, he never suggested I assume at least part of the cost. (If he was worried that rather than do that, I'd quit, he needn't have: my faith in the process was so ingrained that I probably would have cheerfully forked over my own money despite what I knew about my behavior on the couch; on the other hand, perhaps spending my own money would have spurred me to do more to overcome my resistance.)

"Is it helping?" my father would murmur when I gave him the bill each month, but then he'd start writing the check without waiting for an answer. Periodically I'd feel so guilty about wasting his money that when something that I brought up during my hour actually made me cry, I'd also be almost pleased, as if my tears were some kind of proof that I was at least "trying."

Whenever I cried, I'd secretly go through what I thought of as my "snot ritual":

Realizing that I'd again "forgotten" a handkerchief, I'd lie there in a quandary because in order to get a Kleenex from the box on my analyst's desk, I'd have to get up from the couch.

But: According to theory, impulses such as these should be analyzed rather than acted upon.

And: Those patients for whom the box of Kleenex was readily available—the ones who sat in the chair by the desk instead of lying down on the couch—were those poor souls who, because of the nature of their psychological problems or because they didn't have the money, were treated with psychotherapy rather than with psychoanalysis. The looser and more supportive methods of the former—with the more "human" therapist, seen only once or twice a week, occasionally even giving a bit of avuncular advice, were easier to take but also more superficial than those of the latter; palliative rather than curative. In the analytic hierarchy, psychotherapy patients were Cub Scouts rather than Marines; or, to flip the coin, more or less second-class citizens.

Snuffling by now and trying to surreptitiously wipe my nose with the back of my hand, I'd think about how disgusting I must look to my analyst sitting silently behind me. Worrying about inadvertently getting some snot on his couch; then fantasizing about acting out and—as surreptitiously as possible—actually doing it, eventually I'd think about all of the other analysands who, over the years, had been lying on my very spot on the very same couch, also crying, some undoubtedly also having "forgotten" a handkerchief. Suddenly I'd start worrying that I was actually lying on some other patient's dried snot!

"Yes?"

Silence.

*   *   *

Although the fact that my analyst and my father shared a profession should have facilitated a potentially rich "transference," I (secretly) resented the coincidence and tended to wish that my father were something like a plumber. As when I'd visit my father's office, at my analyst's I did my best to look only at the feet of the patients who came before and after me; if I'd crossed paths with someone like the apparently much "treated" Marilyn Monroe, I never would have noticed. Like my father's, my analyst's looks and dress were nondescript, but if he'd been a blind, hunchbacked cripple who'd stuttered, I would have done my best to ignore it. And if I'd tripped over one of the toys that his children occasionally left on the walk outside, injuring myself seriously, I would have been the last person to sue. So when his wife left her Bloomingdale's charge card in the patients' bathroom (she must have had her own issues with her husband's profession), although I can't remember whether I brought up the fact that I'd seen it, I'm sure I was resentful at again having my analyst's private life thrust in my face.

"Yes?"

Silence.

Then one day when I was on my way to his office, our eyes met as he was crossing the street with his little daughter, and I heard him call her sweetheart. Doubtless I felt many things: resentful at being exposed to his personal life; moved by his tenderness; jealous because I wasn't his daughter; angry because my father had never used such endearments with me; jealous because my analyst didn't use them with me. But as usual, I wasn't forthcoming. When my hour was nearly up, after undoubtedly waiting patiently for me to mention the encounter, my analyst blurted out, "What about seeing me with my daughter?" What about it?

*   *   *

Despite my attempts to ignore any glimpses into his private life, I couldn't help being aware of my analyst's casual (as compared to my father's) reactions to any intrusions from that life. This tended to make me increasingly critical of the way my father had been, on the one hand, too rigid about any overlap between his professional and personal lives, while on the other, he was also unable to separate these lives and leave his analytic manner at work. ("Did anything happen at school today that upset you?" when I'd complain of a stomachache.) Although it would have been "inappropriate" for me to discuss my treatment with my father, its results doubtless contributed to our deteriorating relationship. (If he suspected why I was so often angry at him, and was bemused, to say the least, that he was paying through the nose to have me berate him; or, more likely, if he was disappointed that I still seemed neurotic; if he just plain old felt bad about losing me; he never let on.) As I was becoming more and more disenchanted, an easy way for me to try to theoretically "get back at him" would have been to quit therapy, but I was still so influenced by his belief in analysis as a panacea that it never occurred to me to at least try something else, like—God forbid—a psychiatrist; or to take a break, if not just quit. Instead, despite my guilt about my resistance, despite my disenchantment with my father and his analytic orientation, I never questioned the validity of the process, and tended to think of my analysis as a kind of vitamin pill that might help and surely couldn't hurt.

*   *   *

Occasionally my analyst, undoubtedly at the end of his rope, would be more aggressive. I'd be lying there silently, thinking something like, "Idea for a short story: Lying silently on her analyst's couch, young woman thinks about writing a story about a young woman who's lying silently on her analyst's couch . . ." Suddenly my analyst would ask what I was thinking. I wouldn't always tell him. (I'm sure that in keeping me on and not even "demoting" me to psychotherapy, my analyst had faith in the process and wasn't just "stealing" my father's money. And as far as money went, I must have been a frustrating enough patient to dispel any doubts my analyst might have had about whether he was truly earning his fee.)

When even I couldn't stand our silences any longer, I'd talk about the new books by "liberated" women novelists like Joan Didion and Margaret Atwood: I was fascinated by the heroine's ironic descriptions of the decor in her analyst's office (the "shrines" to Freud, the "primitive" art); of the men she slept with who couldn't love. But when my analyst tried to get me to try to connect the fiction with my own life, I'd back away. Occasionally I'd bring up a "social" issue like the scantily dressed prostitutes I'd see on Broadway late at night, soliciting suburban drivers; or the mentally ill people from halfway houses whom I'd sit with at my neighborhood Chock Full O'Nuts counter—one of them wore a button that said, "Don't Bother Me, I Can't Cope!" But when my analyst tried to probe how I was coping with the world, I'd basically run away from anything that seemed too . . . personal.

Hour after hour I'd be lying there thinking about something like, were the artifacts decorating his office made in some third world country?

"Yes?"

Silence.

Or I'd be lying there thinking that I enjoyed teaching writing.

"Yes?"

But inhibited by something I'd once heard or read—that a patient wasn't there to dwell on what was right with her—I'd keep it brief.

Occasionally, finally moved by an association, I'd be lying there crying, yet distancing myself from my feelings by thinking something like, "Story idea: Girl thinks about how when you're lying on your analyst's couch and you cry, your tears go in your ears . . ."

"Yes?"

". . . but girl feels too self-conscious because of the way 'tears' rhymes with 'ears' to bring any of this up with her analyst . . ."

If he tried to point out similarities between my reticence and my father's; if he compared my behavior in analysis with my father's reticence at home; I'd think something like, "Hey, buddy! How about leaving them there ironies to us English majors!" and then I'd change the subject.

When he'd occasionally break his silence to ask something like, "Did you ever fantasize about what your father was doing when he was alone with all of those women patients lying on his couch?" I'd do my best to ignore the fact that I was lying on my analyst's couch—more often than not, trying to tug down my miniskirt.

Secretly I suspected that what really interested my analyst were the interconnections between my father's profession and our family; that what made my analyst most frequently break his silence would be to "casually" say something like, "Let's go back to the way your classmates teased you by saying things like 'Analysts are crazy!' or 'Analysts' children are crazy!'" Secretly feeling that what he secretly wanted was information that would help him be a better father, I resented having my life used as a cautionary tale. I also secretly resented having my father's hard-earned money used to help my analyst's children not only monetarily but also emotionally. Even though I was beginning to see things like my father's sending us all to various therapists as him basically passing the buck rather than trying to help us deal with our problems, perhaps the difficulties I experienced with my own analysis made me (grudgingly) give him credit for never being too proud to go back into treatment himself. Of course all this would have been fertile material to analyze, if only I'd been able to do it.

I also secretly felt that my analyst was secretly interested in gossip about my friend Tanya's affair with her (former) analyst, and although I worried that Tanya and I were drifting apart—they were living together and I rarely saw her alone—in a way I was also relieved not to have much new information about their affair.

Silence.

*　*　*

One day a repressed memory surfaced! When I was around three my parents were separated and so I was staying with my grandparents. One afternoon as my grandfather was napping in his study, I tiptoed in and took all of his pills from the medicine bottle that was on the table beside him. When he woke up and discovered that they were missing, he and my grandmother rushed me to the hospital, where I had my stomach pumped. This was as much as I'd been told about the incident, which I barely remembered—until, one day when I was lying on the couch these many years later, I suddenly remembered very clearly what had really happened that afternoon: Looking around my grandfather's dark study for something to do, I had indeed taken the capsules; but after carefully emptying the powder into the toilet, I'd held the gellike containers under warm tap water, and then had done nothing more than play with the rubbery mass for a little while before guiltily flushing everything away. My panicked grandparents must not have asked many questions, and afraid to admit what I'd done, I probably hadn't understood enough of what was going to happen to me to admit the truth.

"Oh my God, Karen, what happened?"

Silence.

In the end, I'd had my stomach pumped for no reason. Potentially rich material—perhaps I'd unconsciously wanted to make my grandparents look negligent so I could live with at least one of my estranged parents, who must have united to rush to my bedside.

My analyst must have visibly brightened, and my guilt at wasting my father's money must have been at least temporarily assuaged, but doubtless sooner rather than later, I changed the subject.

Fifty minutes a day, five days a week.

Another day I was lying on the couch musing about how although I liked chicken, for some reason I disliked chicken salad—my usual chitchat—when my analyst suddenly interrupted to ask what kind of sandwiches my Aunt Ruth had made me for my dreaded return journey home; and suddenly I remembered what they were. Impressed with the analytic process, I probably made a harder stab than usual at fighting my resistance, for a while.

Fifty minutes a day, five days a week, eleven months a year . . .

And then suddenly one day, I acted out. Sitting at a luncheonette before my hour, suddenly realizing I'd be late if I didn't get moving, I had my coffee put into a cardboard container with a lid and then took it with me to my analyst's, somehow "forgetting" analytic theory, which stipulates that the analysand should resist the "instant gratification" that comes from doing things like smoking or drinking during the hour; instead, he or she should let frustration build like steam in a kettle, and analyze why he or she had felt the impulse to act out in the first place. But when my analyst came to the waiting room as usual to usher me into his office, his tie and demeanor neutral, there I was with my container of coffee! Looking at it quizzically, he must have tried not to brighten visibly. Suddenly realizing the full significance of what I'd done, I must have wished I could "undo" having brought it in the first place. Although analysts tend to be atheists, he must have felt like falling on his knees.

Walking ahead of him into his office, I must have been tempted to murmur "Oops!" and then casually toss the full container in the wastebasket, before casually heading for the couch as if nothing untoward had happened. On my way to the couch, I must have held the container before me as if I were carrying something like a warm turd.

Adding to the general awkwardness of the situation, in my impetuosity it hadn't dawned on me that I wouldn't be able to drink lying down without spilling coffee all over myself and the couch. (Did I imagine coffee stains mingling on the discreet tweed fabric with the snot that I'd previously wiped off my hand? Did I associate to Tanya's analyst's semen on his couch? Or, speaking of semen on the couch . . .) It probably hadn't occurred to me that in order to actually drink my coffee I'd have to sit in the chair near my analyst's desk, the very chair that was only used by those patients who were merely in psychotherapy.

I can't remember whether I defiantly finished my coffee (it must have tasted like ashes) and then went to the couch, or if I sat there and just let it get cold while I tried to chat as if nothing unusual were going on. Perhaps, trying to distract my analyst from my act, I freely associated. Or maybe after finishing my coffee I casually threw the container in the wastebasket, missed, picked it up, and deposited it carefully, making my way nonchalantly over to the couch. Could it be that after finishing my coffee I simply decided to say the hell with it, and stayed in my chair for the rest of my hour? I do remember that afterward, both my analyst and I referred to that incident as "the coffee episode."

Fifty minutes a day, five days a week, eleven months a year.

With one exception: One winter day when I arrived at my usual time I rang the bell, but my analyst didn't buzz me in. There was no sign of the patient who preceded me, and when I went to a phone-booth and dialed his number, I got a busy signal. Confused and upset, I went home and tried to get through for the next few days, but still couldn't reach him. When I finally made contact, he said that he'd told me he'd been away on vacation (and coincidentally that his phone had been out of order). I was sure that he hadn't told me; that in informing his various other patients, he'd somehow forgotten to let me know. But he insisted that I'd been so threatened by his "abandoning" me that I'd repressed the fact that he'd be away. I was furious that he assumed the problem was mine.

Of course, no matter who was right or wrong, analyzing my reactions could have been fruitful. . . .

Eleven months a year, for most of my twenties.

*   *   *

Although my analysis wasn't a total waste of time (focusing on myself for fifty minutes a day, no matter how superficially, couldn't

have hurt; and my analyst certainly did what he could to help), I probably would have done better if I'd paid for my therapy myself and
gone to someone with less fancy credentials. No doubt a psychiatric
social worker would have suggested sooner that I shape up or simply
terminate.

Vested Interests

Geraldine A. J. Sanford

I would come, a question mark in your chair,
poised for answers I now comprehend as
contrary to your vested interests
to disclose, the split of your loyalty
weighted toward your affiliation,
provoking your chattering distractions
from the main issues, such as the motive
behind those fractures of soul and spirit
to which I had been subjected, whether
or not for folly of falling victim
to split diagnoses, more opportune
to blame on the patient, such physicians
beyond error, of course, born deities,
sprung from the loins of Hippocrates, their
certificates clutched in their baby fists.

Putdown

Geraldine A. J. Sanford

I put the needs of others before my own,
you chided, putting down the nurturing
on which I thrived before the constriction
of your negating therapeutic touch,
putting down my intellect, too, cum laude
or not, both my honors and my honor,
snatching away all the hunches on which
I might grow, and bloom, blowing your blurring
genie smoke over the enlightenment
of the genie before, putting that down
as some vague error you promised you would
not repeat, and you didn't, showing me
instead to this humbling place, the dunce stool
in the corner, shrugging off my wisdoms
as effrontery to your agenda,
condemning me back to the Underland
you led me into that first November
we met, under prejudicial auspices,
setting me up for the MMPI
profile of your choice, an ideal frame
for that feigned image you tainted of me,
stretching on a canvas of my skin and bone,
that most flagrant denial of this self
you do not choose to see or to believe.

Is She Really Listening?

Anna Mills

I came to therapy each week as to a shrine. I walked up to the back door of the college health center, breathless and hopeful, believing that pieces of me would weave together as I sat there talking. I would walk out grounded—sometimes in pain, sometimes happy, but always closer to the truth of my condition. The words "eating disorder" comforted me. I had a right to be there.

Anne had long skirts and wavy hair and wore little makeup. She was professional and kind. She would sweep out of the office, flashing me a smile, so that I wondered if she had some secret source of joy.

Entering her office, I took time to arrange my coat on the chair and situate my backpack. I told myself to relax, to take my time and not be intimidated. Anne sat, hands folded in her lap. Then something closed off inside me. My body tensed, and I assumed my usual position, hunched forward, arms wrapped around my belly. She was waiting, therefore I could not speak. I wanted her to speak first, to tell me what the terms were.

I always longed for someone to listen to me deeply. I might be silent for hours, prompting my friends to talk, but when someone began to ask me questions, my words flew out of control. I talked until I had figured something out. I held onto that new piece of myself. So I yearned for responses, questions, affirmations from Anne. I hated her silence.

What did this eating disorder mean? Why did I keep focusing all of my energy on my size and my eating, even after I knew the answers? What was this secret language telling me about my life? I knew there was something disturbed about my relationships with men. Why were my feelings so frightened, obsessive, and ambivalent? How could I feel comfortable with my body and my sexuality around men? I wanted my therapist to take me seriously as a person capable of learning something about this condition. The words "eating disorder" were like runes I kept hidden and could not decipher. They were a force I held in awe. I wanted to read them the way you read a sacred text over and over, seeking a new understanding that would transform my life.

Anne's style when she did speak was to soothe and comfort me. The week before winter break, she brought me a list of strategies to use while I was home. They were written in a flowing, lovely script. "Read a book. Call a friend. Go for a walk. Write. Be aware of anger. Be aware of sadness."

I smiled faintly, gratefully, and began to worry. As sweet, calming, and Zen as these thoughts were, they seemed to conjure up some other woman than myself. To me, my eating disorder meant I could not pacify or tame my hunger. I could not silence or quiet it by nurturing myself like a baby. I had to know what it meant; I had to give my hunger a voice in my life. I had to uncover its rage and power and set them to work.

Anne gave me no clues. Neither did she reflect back to me the contradictory, confused ideas I was putting forward. How could I figure out who I was without feedback? By not revealing her responses, she left me vulnerable and herself untouchable. I wanted a reassuring, insightful mirror, but the image she gave me was cloudy, vague, always disappearing. I talked compulsively and anxiously, never sure what my real point was. She seemed to accept everything. She listened, my words were swallowed up, and then they disappeared. In the face of her kind, poised silence, I felt ugly and selfish. I wished I could be as securely feminine as she was. I wished for her silent power, her serenity.

Each time I questioned my therapy, I wondered if I were blind. Maybe I was really angry at my mother. Maybe Anne intended me to be angry and knew that it would cure me. How could I know what I needed, since I didn't understand my disorder? My anger was another symptom, another clue to my neurosis. I suspected that Anne would always be right in the end.

At the same time, I began to articulate the anger. It flashed in and out of my mind. Why should Anne be certain of herself, of her place in the world, of her rightness, just because she was silent and I was talking? Why should she be the expert? Wasn't I the expert, since I was unraveling this complicated text of my eating disorder, this story about myself?

The more I learned about the meaning of my hunger, the more political I became. Late in my therapy, it seemed evident to me that eating disorders are a cultural and a political phenomenon. They are epidemic among women because of the self-sacrificing, self-effacing roles we are expected to play, and because our bodies, our sexuality, and our worth are defined in relation to men. Anne never discounted the political meaning of eating disorders, but she never responded to my tentative ideas.

One year after leaving therapy, I came out as a lesbian. As I recognized my own desires, my eating problems virtually disappeared. I no longer focused much energy on food or weight, and I ate freely. Whereas other women had once inspired my jealousy and self-criticism, they now inspired attraction. I was no longer afraid of my own appetite or of what it might betray about me. The connection was strong and uncanny.

No one—not my closest friends, my lesbian aunt, or Anne—had guessed that I might be attracted to women. No one would have imagined that there was a huge epiphany waiting for me; that the language of my eating disorder could have such a dramatic, unexpected meaning. I do not blame Anne for not realizing that I was a lesbian, but therapy with her did not allow me to achieve that realization myself.

Thinking back, I believe that I worried about her reaction to my unnamed difference. I wrote in my journal, "I'm threatened by her femininity—it doesn't feel like she's friendly." Her thin body, demure skirts, her makeup and her understanding, her cautious, soft tone and restrained manner, and the constant half smile and bright eyes made me feel invisible. Somehow she seemed too established, too satisfied and definite about her femininity to understand my struggles.

I don't believe Anne was actively homophobic. I am convinced, however, that she did have reservations about something she sensed in me. She may not have consciously felt it, but she may have been uncomfortable with the area I was negotiating between straight and lesbian awareness, and the implications of my growing dissatisfaction with men. Whether it was fear or ignorance or a lack of vocabulary, she didn't engage me in my own attempt to wrestle with the meanings of my eating and sexuality.

After I came out, I went back to see Anne, determined to cruise into her office as the survivor turned expert. I could find very little in the literature about the link between homophobia and eating disorders, and I had begun to develop my own theory. Anne seemed interested in my views. She said eating disorders were about many different things. Some women acquired them due to events in their lives. Sometimes they would establish the behavior pattern and be unable to escape it. She asked me many questions about my current life and emotions.

Again I felt my voice and sense of personhood dissolve in the office I had entered interested in a peer discussion of treatment methods and ideologies. I left confused, seeing myself as a patient again, someone whose words must always be traced back to a particular neurosis.

To me, the most frightening thing about my therapy with Anne was that neither of us recognized we were mismatched. I believe our socialization as women who want to nurture and please others contributed to this oversight. Perhaps an even stronger influence was the dynamic of therapy itself. As long as I clung to the belief that she was the expert, I would not fully trust my own insights. Both she and I hoped that my "resistance" was just another clue to my "disease."

In the end, I was determined to make my "shrine" exactly what I needed. I struggled to define myself despite her method and became clearer about myself and my beliefs. I left subsequent sessions satisfied and happy, feeling that by resisting her I had created a small breathing space, a place where I made sense.

Yet I continue to believe that a different therapist might have worked better. Not a perfect therapist who could guess my attraction to women before I could, but one who was comfortable and self-aware enough to respond to me honestly. I needed someone who could encourage my tentative thoughts about eating disorders and women's roles, a mentor who could nurture questions about my sexuality, and actively help me be aware of the possibilities, including eating disorders as a struggle for identity.

The year after I left therapy, I learned a technique for commenting on creative writing. The technique was simple: Reserve judgment and listen, so you can reflect back. In my writing class, we discussed every story in terms of what effect it had on us, what its themes were, and what its meaning was for us. Through discussion, the stories emerged as living beings, with personality, quirks, inexplicable points, and clumsiness or elegance. Each story became a living thing, not a number on a scale of excellence. When my own stories were to be discussed, I looked forward to feedback fearfully for days. Once in the class, listening to people discuss my autobiographical stories, I wanted be anywhere else, and I wondered why I put myself through such a grueling experience. But I took notes and carried away realizations about myself, outside pictures that helped me see myself more calmly, in spite of my embarrassment. That first year after my therapy, I spilled everything onto the page and waited for it to be reflected back, so I could piece it together, smile or groan, and continue on, with a sense of my own importance and complexity. In this therapy I was finally the expert, as well as the author, writing my own life.

Sometimes I would see Anne in town. I took pleasure in waving to her, knowing that she would not acknowledge me otherwise. She could not seem to meet me face-to-face as a person with whom she had worked and shared explorations and insights. Maybe she was trying to protect my privacy. Yet I did not need to be protected. I existed, whole and often happy, outside of her space. I felt free, master of myself. In that way, I liked her.

We Go a Little Over the Hour

Kathleen M. Kelley

what pained me most
about my mother's wintry gift
for silent, long suffering
was its loneliness.

my client has written a poem for today—
what she remembers:
the last warm conversation with her own mother
the casual way she got into the car that morning
the fatal rumor spreading through the schoolyard
while the other mountain kids held their breath
the hole burned into the highway
the truck driver's phone call to her family
his failed brakes
(his name, when I ask, gone up in smoke),
the coroner handing her what remained.
she tried to clean it for her father's sake,
ash burned into the wedding ring
later, under her tires
a daily bump left from the clumsy repair
Christmas presents under the bed,
the names of all the children on unwrapped boxes:
Virginia, Catherine, Peter,
Matthew, Jonathan, Marie.

as we speak it is quiet and my client's face is flushed
she is rocking and the clock is ticking
the reminiscence wraps around us like a ribbon
people ask me how I bear listening to endless sorrow

I can listen to anything, wrapped around like ribbon
I can listen to it all as long as I know it makes a difference:
my body's audible breathing, soft sounds, quivering heart

I can take the time we need as well
to read her poem out loud
though we go a little over the hour.

Suite 506

Barbara Shooltz Kendzierski

I love this room.
I hate this room.
I feel cradled and connected.
I feel isolated and broken.
I see progress.
I see loss.
I see what might have been
and was not.

I hear poetry and prayer.
I hear panic and despair.
I touch blackness, pain and rot.
I touch my soul.
I love this room.
I hate this room.

I sense your humanness,
your presence.
I sense your strength,
your need.
I love you.
I fear you.
You disturb my life.
You reflect possibility.

If who I am can be,
if what I need can be,
how can I settle for what is?
Why do I return

to feel confronted,
to feel discomforted?
Because.
I hate this room.
I love this room.

Escaping the Cabin

Adrienne Ross

One January night before starting the antidepressant Paxil, I had a dream: *I am in a log cabin, an infant strapped to my chest. Outside a violent, swirling snowstorm howls through a conifer forest. Sentries in dark fur coats stand knee-deep in the snow guarding the cabin. They have no weapons. There is a civil war. Our side has lost the battle. The victors will come to kill us. A woman sentry advises us not to leave the cabin or let the victors enter. Someone else advises us to fight. We have no weapons. If we stay in the cabin, the invaders will burn it. If we fight, they will kill us. I decide to leave. I trudge through the thick, clinging snow and think that if the choice is survival or a lost cause, I'll leave and survive.*

My dream clawed its way to consciousness during a winter of broken fertility and blocked creativity. That same winter my therapist decided I was depressed, and in need of herself and medication to guide me. I was in a crisis but not one either of us understood.

Three years earlier, a routine internal exam had led to an abrupt, unexpected diagnosis of endometriosis, a disease of the reproductive system. Surgery revealed a diffuse, murky mass spread across my uterus and one remaining ovary. In order to protect what remained of my fertility, I went on a six-month hormone regimen that induced a temporary, artificial menopause. In the three years that followed I traveled abroad and within, started a business, parted with lovers and explored new ones, all the while shedding skin, identities, certainties. Questions haunted me. How could I have been so sick for so long and not know it? What else didn't I know about myself?

All you come back with is a story. The words flared in my mind one chill, rain-stroked January dawn before going on the Paxil. A well-published nature writer, I needed to return to my tales of urban peregrines and autumn migrations. A New York City literary agent was waiting for the first chapter of a book that would restart a career stalled by illness. The well-traveled streams of my imagination went suddenly bone dry. *All you come back with is a story.* Week after week, I clamped my jaws shut on those words, broke pens, gnashed teeth, cried during the night and the day.

I believed I could triumph over the changes forced on me. If only from sheer will, I could have the child I wanted. If only because I wanted to, I could continue to write within the known, safe realms of salmon and cedar. I dreamt of being the only survivor on the *Titanic.* I dreamt of meeting crones by a hearth fire. My dreams were stark prophecies that the story I came back with would not be the one I wanted. I didn't understand my dreams. Neither did my therapist.

This pain is not what you think, my therapist would say, her Shirley Temple curls bobbing as her plump face nodded in emphasis. We sat in a narrow room. Between us was a mahogany coffee table with a clock gleaming red digits, a bouquet of purple statice in a burnt umber Mexican vase, and the requisite box of tissues. *Look to your past for its reasons,* she would say, her brown eyes soft, sad behind gold-rimmed glasses.

After each session I would walk through a nearby park. Everywhere mothers pushed strollers, their infants and toddlers alert to a brave new world of Douglas fir trees and in-line skaters. To mother a child. An essential part of humanity, of myself, I longed to experience. Returning home, I'd force myself to lift pen to empty page and write line after leaden, repetitive line about sockeye salmon returning to local creeks to mate, lay their eggs, and die before their young are born. Day after day, page after page of crossed-out words, between ringing phones and glimpses of cedar waxwings in barren Japanese maples, unanswered questions stalked me. How could I live if I couldn't create, not in words, not in children? Why had I worked so hard for either, only to lose both? How was I to live now and for the rest of my life?

My therapist had her own answers. Therapy's core dogma is that the therapist sees what the client cannot. Like all dogma, it rests on faith alone. My therapist would lean back into a fluted armchair embroidered with faux floral needlepoint, her zaftig body draped in brown cotton drawstring pants, bulky tan pullovers, and Birkenstocks. She would shake her head. No, I was not feeling enormous, unavoidable grief over being childless. It was not even a child I wanted. Rather, my inner child was reacting to the inadequate mothering I had received. Never mind my national publications and writing awards. *Your creativity is at the stage of a six-month-old,* she would coo in a contralto voice. *You're really just a child. A child. I will love that vulnerable inner child even if you can't. I will defend her.*

"We cannot live in a world interpreted for us by others. An interpreted world is not home . . ." pleaded Hildegaard von Bingen centuries earlier. To my therapist, there was always another fragmented recollection, another half-recalled, distant conversation that was more important than my present life challenges. Elusive, omnipotent, shadowy, the past eclipsed without illuminating my daily crisis of meaning. The more immersed I became in her interpretations of my past, the more alienated I became from the power—imperfect, limited—which only exists in the present. As the weeks progressed, my doubts grew.

One day, I told my therapist how during Shabbat services the rabbi had asked the congregation to close our eyes and see ourselves as God sees us. A vision had flared behind my closed eyes: I stood ankle-deep in a vast, glimmering turquoise ocean, my body bathed in gold light, in joy, swollen in pregnancy. My therapist leaned toward me, closed her fingers over her bronze Venus of Willendorf medallion, looked deeply into my eyes, and said: *This vision is of your inner child, your innocent child self, waiting to come into the light.* I was stunned. I wanted a child. My story silenced, I cried without words, without sounds.

There were other days when I sank into the mauve floral print love seat and said, *This is making my life worse, not better.* I wanted to write again. I wanted to reestablish the trust in my body, in myself, that had been ruptured by illness. *I am a grown woman,* I would insist, my teeth gritted. *No,* my therapist would respond. *You're really just a child. Try drawing with crayons. Try cooking the foods you ate as a child, tapioca pudding or spaghetti and meatballs. I will keep speaking up for your child self even if you won't. Let her thrive.*

I don't want this to continue, I finally began to say, pushing aside the offered box of tissues. *I want to end the therapy.*

Suddenly, she agreed. The therapy wasn't working. She had tried everything she knew. Somatic releasing. Eye movement desensitization and reprocessing. Talking. Process therapy. All the things that had worked so well for her. If the old joys of words and nature brought no pleasure, if I could see no meaning in my life, if I wasn't responding to therapy, there was only one explanation.

Depression, she said. She leaned back against the armchair's wide, padded back and smiled. Her index finger tap-tap-tapped her plump thigh. *Depression. There are medications. They only help. There's no harm.*

Depression. I tried to fit that word into my mouth as if it came from behind my tongue. Depression. A biochemical disturbance in the brain. A too-fast, too-complete synaptic absorption of serotonin. A synthesis of trauma and neurotransmitter imbalance. I would later learn that whether from biological or social reasons, depression has long been a "woman's ailment." We are far more likely than men to be labeled depressed and to be the recipients of mood-altering drugs such as Prozac or Paxil. I would come to learn, too, that depression isn't sadness or grief, but the inability to feel sadness or grief, bittersweet longing, frivolous joy, even impetuous gratitude at being alive. Yet my feelings were closer than I wanted.

Underneath my dream cabin rolled a turbulent river. Seeping through layers of earth, firmament, bone, skin, self were emotions, raw, unwanted, no longer contained. I woke sobbing over grief I thought long forgotten. I tore editors' brief rejection letters into tiny, jagged shreds, my stoic acceptance long gone. While meditating, my mind filled with images of shimmering crimson snakes swiftly uncoiling from my ankles, slinking up my crossed legs, my naked chest, my shoulders, their quick, forked tongues cleaning my ears. Snakes: consorts of the mother goddess, ancient symbols of wisdom and rebirth.

I want my own freedom, I wrote one gray morning in my journal, *freedom from my own rules, my limits, my shoulds.* Then came the next words: *All you come back with is a story.* I slammed the journal shut. I refused to make this story real by writing it down with words. No other stories came.

". . . part of the terror is to take back our own listening. To use our own voice. To see with our own light . . ." wrote von Bingen long ago. The more I heard my therapist's voice, the harder it became to hear my own. The more I tried to dam that underground river, the more it jumped its channels to rise in sobbing, in desperate urges for solitude, in the first incoherent stammering of my unwanted story, in sharp, sudden rages. The angrier I became, the more urgently my therapist would grip her chair's floral brocade armrests and say: *Go on the medication. You are depressed.*

Depression. A name: power's stubborn, gripping root. Naming assigns identity, essence, self. Like most Jews, I have an innate regard for names. Jews have no name for God, that source behind creation. Instead, there are many designators, perhaps the most common being Hashem: The Name.

Depression. This name gave me a reason not to make cold calls to revive my floundering business, not to put on a red dress and matching lipstick for a swing dance, not to heed my dream's warning, not to decipher my sorrow's rejected message. It gave me a reason not to listen to what I didn't want to hear: a sibilant inner whisper that I would be childless, a frightening, seductive roar behind my creative silence.

Could I really say this wasn't my name? Once I had thought I was well only to have the endometriosis silently ravage my left ovary, devastate my fertility. Could I trust myself to know when I was sick, when I was well? Perhaps this strange crisis was another hidden, growing darkness. In the end, it was the endometriosis that convinced me I had to at least try the antidepressants.

The Paxil took effect immediately, although not in any way my doctor or therapist had mentioned. Nausea began on my second day. Bitter vomit would rise up in my throat, gagging me. Dry mouth followed. I could hardly eat, yet my body bloated. Sheer exhaustion came next. I pushed fingernails in my palms to keep from falling asleep at client meetings. I nodded off in mid-sentence at my science and spirituality discussion group, groggily waking up to a circle of stunned, annoyed faces. Erotic desire died. The flesh between my legs became wooden, inert, a brittle uprooted tree.

Much later, I would learn that what I was experiencing were routine side effects of selective serotonin reuptake inhibitors such as Paxil and Prozac. Neither my doctor nor therapist warned of other common side effects such as the inability to think or remember clearly, apathy, a loss of spontaneity and, ironically, other conditions quite common to depression.

Stay on the Paxil, my therapist urged. *It will only help you.* I refused. It was my first small step into those snowy woods. Another drug was found: Wellbutrin. Then came another tentative step toward whatever was far past that blinding snowstorm. I left therapy.

At first the Wellbutrin was benign. I could stay awake. I could talk coherently to clients. I could feel erotic joy, if not desire. I could find myself in my body. Shortly after beginning the drug, I spent a weekend at an ecstatic dance workshop. My body, free to follow its own moves, flowed me through chaos, joy, stillness. My body spoke. An inner command for silence fell quiet. Censorship gone, in its place was a void waiting for creation.

The following Monday I had to get away—from my cobwebbed office, my darkened basement rooms, from this looming vastness, from whatever was fast approaching the cabin in my dream.

I drove hard and fast north from Seattle to the Skagit Valley marshes. Beauty never failed me there, no matter how harsh or predatory. The Interstate 5 highway was slick with winter rain. Above me was a brooding sky, steel gray as a gun barrel. Stars, moon, clouds, sunlight, glory rays were hidden by a soft wall of rain. The highway curved on to country roads of mud and gravel that led to a wildlife refuge.

My steps shattered thin ice crusts. I tramped across black mud, past wind-brittle logs, the sun-worn bones of long gone forests. I sat butt cold on a rain-damp, moss-encrusted log. I screamed to the silence, to the wind, to God: *Why this world?* Why this world of empty wombs, unwanted stories? I cried what I still couldn't say but already knew. No matter how deep my desires, how strong my hopes, there would be no children in my life.

If I couldn't have children, I could still write. Except my beloved world of tawny winged owls swooping into twilight was no longer whispering in my ear. A new world was; a still unknown tongue. *All you come back with is a story.* If I wanted to write, I would have to put the old pens down, follow my creative intuition as it cut tracks across new landscapes of eroticism, spirituality, family.

I screamed. *Why? Why? Why?* Bitter words in a sharp wind. My tears streaked with rain. *Why? Why? Why?* until I suddenly felt an eerie, primal, irrational gratitude to be alive in this world of coyote tracks, snow geese rising from mud like white camellias, a great blue heron's stillness a Buddha would envy. To live in this numinous, ineluctable world was to admit pain, to find meaning in broken dreams, joy in an unwanted fate.

I stayed on the marsh until rain gave way to night. Orion rose. Wind chilled me but only skin deep. Trumpeter swans flew with moonlight between their feathers. Wing beats and their calls broke the silence.

There were no more days like that, once the Wellbutrin took effect. I slept free from dreams. I never knew if crones confronted me before I woke, if besieged cabins were finally destroyed. "The unconscious wants truth," writes poet Adrienne Rich. "It ceases to speak to those who want something else more than truth."*

I spent hours staring into my computer screen's glare, stabbing keys with slow fingers, trying and failing to write grant proposals for my withering business. My notebooks were filled with blank pages. Jackets and junk mail lay piled on my writing table. Words backed up deep in my throat, quicksilver fish quivering behind a logjam. I felt no sudden happiness at white star blossoms on gnarled cherry tree branches. Tears dried up. Anger shriveled. Exhaustion remained. A slowness of body and mind left me without spirit to dance, concentration to read. Recipes, shopping lists, and other simple instructions confounded me no matter how often I had them repeated.

Each day I swallowed a dull yellow, fingernail-sized pill of self-doubt. *What was wrong with me that I needed these pills? Did I even need them at all? Were they really helping?* Days became weeks. I remained calm in my despair, uninvolved, as if my life was an abandoned town I visited from time to time.

The Wellbutrin was doing all an antidepressant can do: altering my mood while leaving the conditions of my life unchanged. Like the soma-laden workers in *Brave New World,* I adjusted to a stunted life. Compared to this, the crying and sudden rages, the raw gratitude to be alive, the enigmatic dreams were all gifts from my deepest mysteries and desires.

One late March morning, I left the orange vial of pills in my medicine cabinet. The next morning the Wellbutrin remained tucked behind aspirin and moisturizing cream. It stayed there the next morning as well. I stepped farther into the woods; only now the wind was abating, the snow no longer falling.

Days turned into weeks. Dreams returned. I could cry again. I didn't try to stop the tears. I was starved for feelings. Slowly, I could act again. I made the cold calls needed to restore my business. Clients returned. I moved from my dreary basement rooms to a sunlit apartment. I fell in love.

---

*Adrienne Rich. *On Lives, Secrets, and Silence.* Boston: W.W. Norton & Co., 1975, p. 187.

One cold spring afternoon on a Whidbey Island beach, my back against a wind-peeling log, my feet in the chill sand, I wrote a letter to God. *God,* I wrote, *all this pain and for what?* Once I accepted my sorrow as real, I could discover its lesson, express its meaning in my own words. Pain no longer mastered me. The world's inevitable beauty returned.

Faith, I wrote, *I'd like that, to believe there's more than what I can know.* A poem. A prayer. The first soundings of a newly burnished voice. In the weeks that followed, I wrote without grace, without gratitude of the last three years. By denying my story, therapy had created silence, and silence is the heart of censorship. The lost hours in the therapist's white-walled office, the dazed months on drugs had been an initiation: silence was no longer possible. If you refuse to speak your story, someone else will put the words in your mouth.

My words revealed a deeper wisdom of my body and a fuller appreciation of myself as a woman independent of whether I could have children. My words, too, revealed a restored trust in myself, and a more intimate, problematic relationship with Hashem. Notebooks filled with story. Story became home; my walking ground; my wisdom. My once-barren future became fertile ground for creativity and exploration. The last three years became an unwanted lesson, but one worth learning.

I believe we are too quick to label as "depression" life's inevitable sorrows, its unfairness and randomness, its spiritual challenges. Perhaps depression can be cured with a pill, but life cannot. When suffering is gone, so too is the unexpected freedom to go beyond what life is supposed to be and on to a greater appreciation of what life is. I wonder how many people on antidepressants are truly medically depressed? How many simply feel heartfelt pain and live in a society that tolerates nothing less than happiness?

What are the stories we are losing?

Therapy

Celia Jeffries

Chris wants to kill herself. She says she has the pills. Yesterday she was fired from her job and today she says she sees no way out. "It's over," she says. Actually she says very little. We question her and watch as the answers make their way slowly, ever so slowly, from her staring eyes and her silent mouth. She was given a choice—find a less demanding job in the nursing home where she works the night shift, or apply for disability. We are not surprised. She was hospitalized this summer and given electroshock therapy.

When I first joined the group I used to look over at her and wonder why she bothered to come. She never spoke, never even moved her large body from the position she took when she first sat down. When someone asked her a direct question it was painful to watch her try to respond, like a paraplegic willing the leg to move, all that effort concentrated on a single body part. I would hold my breath while she struggled to open her mouth, to respond. I would have to stifle my impulse to hand her the words. What is the matter with her? I would think, becoming angry at her for taking up so much time and space. I just can't fathom the depths of her despair. After years of meeting with us once a week, she revealed today that she had been in therapy since the age of twenty-one.

"What sent you to therapy to begin with?" I ask.

"I overdosed," she answers.

She is fifty-two now. So many years of emotional turmoil she has lived. Yet she sits like a washing machine, self-contained, quiet, with no indication of the frenetic thrashing inside. When they hospitalized her did they find the dirty laundry, all twisted and soaked and stuck in mid-cycle? Did they just rattle her a bit to readjust the load, and send her off with the remains of her fifty-two-year-old wardrobe still churning inside?

Electroshock therapy. It sounds so barbaric, so outdated, not something that would be done to a person in the 1990s. They did it to Jack

Nicholson in the movies. They did it to Anne Sexton, the poet. And they did it to my mother, when I was five. Of course I didn't know that until years later, long after the fear and shock of finding someone else standing in my mother's body, a body with foreign eyes that terrorized me at the dinner table.

Now I look at Chris and think of the piece of wood between the teeth, the arms and legs strapped to the table, the electrodes attached to the body. And I think of my mother, always walking on the edge. The wrong remark, the wrong look would set her off into rage or remorse. There is no edge to Chris. I've never seen her angry, or sad or happy. And yet she is very much one of us. When she's not here we miss her, and tell her so. When she does speak, we listen attentively. She is such a silent witness, always sitting. Calm. Quiet. Watching but not judging. Perhaps we should have turned to her more often, jabbed at her, pushed her to her own edge, instead of leaving that to the technicians in the locked ward.

I am perplexed by such despair. I sit here not sure if she will be alive next week, if she will show up, or if we will wait for the announcement that she is no longer with us.

I am perplexed by the therapy process.

"It's time to end now," Dr. Johnson says.

And we all ask her to call him if she's desperate, and we all ask her if she's OK to drive, and we all walk calmly to our cars although it's quite clear that someone who wants to kill herself is not OK to drive. Someone who wants to kill herself should not be told, "It's time to end now."

Preview

Nancy A. McMichael

We sit on a wooden bench near the front hallway and I try not to notice the hairs growing on her chin. Long hairs, almost an inch long. I know what they are from—shock treatments. I don't know how I know this; I just do. I don't even know how I know she had shock treatments. Perhaps some of my knowledge comes to me through osmosis—invisible pollen floating in the air, landing on my skin, seeping into my pores, absorbed by the cells in my blood that carry it directly to my heart.

She sits round-shouldered, head bowed, chin resting on her chest, and rocks back and forth. Her hands lie limp in her lap, fingers slightly swollen, nails long. Brown freckle-like spots dot the backs of her hands.

"Do you need anything?" I ask, watching her hands.

"They said I ran down the hall and climbed in bed with a man."

Her words scatter across the floor like dust balls caught in a passing breeze. I sit quietly and wait, thinking maybe she is telling me a story about one of the other patients. Someone she has met. Someone who sleeps in the next bed, the next ward. She rubs her thumb over the brown spots on the back of her left hand; her thumbnail digs into her skin.

Someone knocks over a chair on the other side of the room. I look. A woman wearing a baggy housedress and ratty terry cloth slippers curses at the wooden chair lying at her feet. "God damn it, get out of my way." The words echo off the bare walls.

"I don't remember crawling in bed with that man," my mother says. "Who do you think he was?"

"I don't know," I say, watching an attendant gently lead the woman in the baggy housedress through a door marked "Private." I glance around the room. The lower half of the walls are painted gray, the upper half a dirty white. The floor is a checkerboard pattern of red and black tiles. Vinyl-covered couches and worn-out chairs hug the walls.

A wooden coffee table sits abandoned in the middle of the floor. Three women sit at a wobbly table, playing cards. Three others stare blankly at the television mounted on the wall, the volume turned so low I wonder how they can hear. One woman stands in the corner, as if she has been reprimanded.

Dr. Finley wears a gray suit, a white shirt, and a paisley tie, a tie his kids probably gave him for Father's Day. A thin silver tie bar matches the silver ID bracelet dangling from his wrist. His white shirt is wrinkle free. I bet if I slipped my hands into his pockets I wouldn't find any lint or fuzz or even a stray thread. Most likely I'd find a freshly ironed handkerchief, neatly folded and monogrammed, definitely monogrammed, a Wearever pen, two quarters, three dimes, and a nickel.

The notebook was in the inside breast pocket of his gray jacket, but now he's holding it in his hands, flipping through the pages. I wonder if he is trying to find an alibi. Don't bother, I want to say, it's not there. How could it be? You never noticed her swollen fingers, never even listened to anything the attendants told you.

If I wait a minute, I bet he'll reach inside that same breast pocket and remove the Wearever pen and scribble something on a blank page and then tell me that everything's going to be fine, just fine. See, there he goes, he's reaching inside the pocket. There's the pen. Flick. The point's out. Scribble, scribble. What did I tell you? The pen and notebook are just for show. Like this meeting, it means nothing.

In another five minutes he'll push a button and tell the nurse to record in the logbook that Dr. High-and-Mighty met with daughter of patient 29470. That's all. Just something for the records.

I sit and stare at the edge of Dr. Finley's desk and try not to think or feel. I clear my throat and cross my legs.

"Your mother's doing much better," he says, laying the notebook on his desk. "We've taken her off the medication."

"So now what?" I ask, trying to keep my voice friendly, yet firm.

"We wait and see."

Wait and see? I wonder. "Like you did with the swelling?"

Dr. Finley pauses before speaking. "We weren't sure what was causing the swelling."

"Not sure? The only thing that's changed in this woman's life in the last fourteen years is this new medication and you're not sure what is causing the swelling? You didn't have a clue? What else could it be? A sudden allergic reaction to oatmeal or mashed potatoes or powdered milk?"

Dr. Finley ignores my outburst and reaches for a manila folder on the credenza behind his desk. He leafs through the papers in the folder, pulling one out for a closer inspection, and then slowly, very deliberately, begins to explain, "We had high hopes for this new medication. Some patients have responded to it completely and haven't suffered any side effects." He turns the paper over and runs his finger down a column of numbers. "There is, however, a small percentage of people who have responded only partially or who have found the side effects uncomfortable or intolerable." He lays the folder on his desk and finally looks in my direction. "The drugs we have don't cure the illness," he says. "They control it, and for now they're the best we have."

"But her fingers were so swollen the attendants had to cut off her ring," I say.

"As I said, we had high hopes for this new medication. It has a good success record."

Records! I want to scream. You're going for records now? Sure. Let's just wait and see how puffed up my mother's fingers can really get. Who knows, maybe they'll blow up so big that she'll just float right out the window and then you won't have to bother with her any more.

Dr. Finley takes a deep breath.

"I don't understand," I say, shaking my head. "Why did you wait three whole days?"

"Things just didn't work out as we had hoped," he says. "Your mother was in a particularly vulnerable period, but she's off the medication now and the swelling is receding."

"But her hands were so swollen three days ago that she couldn't even lift a fork to eat."

He snaps the folder shut. "These things happen."

"These things happen?" I scream, unable to control my anger. "THESE THINGS HAPPEN? Not to my mother. Not to MY mother. She's MY MOTHER and don't you ever, EVER EVER EVER forget it!"

In 1983 in the county seat, the same county seat in which sixteen years earlier my grandfather had walked into the courthouse and signed papers to commit my mother to a state mental institution, a doctor diagnosed my mother, who was then fifty-eight, as having an overactive thyroid and prescribed lithium for her. For the first time in over sixteen years, my mother returned to being the person I had known for the first seventeen years of my life. Her recovery, however, was short lived. Two and a half years later she died.

From *Undercurrents*

Martha Manning

October 16, 1990

I am still in disbelief that I am here. The night is eternal, interrupted every fifteen minutes by a nurse doing "checks" with an annoying flashlight. But even without the interruptions, I would not be sleeping. I take a walk around the unit at 2:00 a.m. The fluorescent lights in the hall and nurses' station give an eerie cast to the place. Many people are already up, silently walking the halls in bathrobes and pajamas. We look like ghosts, lost souls inhabiting the shells of our former selves, pacing and counting out the hours till daylight.

In the middle of the night I get a roommate. She is still asleep. I know nothing about her except that she is a cheerleader, because her uniform is the only thing hanging in her closet. Being a depressed cheerleader must be as tough as being a depressed therapist.

We are awakened each morning by loudspeaker. A nurse announces that the *Washington Post* is available for purchase at the nurses' station. We line up groggy and yawning to have what are left of our vital signs assessed by the staff. I run to the phone to call Brian. I get tearful talking to him and can sense his weariness over the phone.

My first ECT is scheduled for tomorrow morning. I am frightened because it sets me on a course from which I cannot turn back. More than losing my memory, I am terrified that I will lose the last remnants of myself.

Immediately after breakfast, I am summoned by loudspeaker to psychodrama group. It is 8:30. Most of us are fighting off a combination of too little sleep and too much medication. Now we are supposed to express our innermost feelings and conflicts through drama. Marie, the psychodrama therapist, is loose and warm. She wears cowboy boots, and on that basis I decide that I like her. However, I have a perverse desire to say that I will participate in this stuff when she shows me hard data on its efficacy in the treatment of severe depression. But I really want the "unaccompanied" privilege, and anyway, I'm too tired to make trouble.

Marie announces that there are two new people in the group. It is apparent who we are because we're the only two people crying. The other woman, Katherine, cut her wrists last night. She sobs and says how much she hates the place and wants to get out. Like newborns who cry in response to the wails of other babies, I burst into tears. Marie places a number of diverse objects in the middle of the room and asks us to choose the ones that most represent how we are feeling. I choose a bright red pillow with a STOP sign on it and a toy sailboat. She asks us to do something I have hated since my first day of kindergarten—"share." We have to go around the room and give the reasons we picked our objects. When my turn comes, I say something inane about wanting the depression to STOP, and wishing I could just sail away.

After psychodrama comes art therapy. Katherine and I are still sniffling. Denise, the art therapist, puts aside her agenda for the moment and allows the people in the group to talk to one another. Barbara tells us how she took an overdose after rounds of cancer chemotherapy and reassures us that she cried continually for a week when she found out that she was going to have to live.

Emmaline, a manager and mother of two girls, adds that she had problems with her lithium and got so high that she was convinced she was going to marry Michael Jordan. She landed in the hospital when she went so far as making the wedding arrangements. The crowning blow came when she modeled her new wedding gown for her husband and sons. She slaps her knee when she finishes her story and laughs so hard she shakes.

Denise invites us to use pastels to draw whatever we want. I draw a huge eye crying and write a poem next to it. Katherine leans over and says, "You don't have to tell me what you do. I know you're a writer." I am relieved not to have to tell people I'm a psychologist and nod my assent.

My friend Pat comes at lunchtime. She brings a painting from her daughter, Suzanne, with a note that says she hopes I'll "stop being sad." Pat sits on my bed while I cry all the tears that have been locked up inside me in the service of survival. She rubs my back as I rest my head on her shoulder.

After lunch I call Lew, who is scheduled to leave for a trip to Italy tomorrow. I let him know that my first treatment is scheduled for tomorrow morning. He has talked to Dr. Samuel and communicates his confidence in him. I wish him a good trip. He wishes me "courage."

It's Going to Be a Great Daypro

Megeen R. Mulholland

Nap and sin
Naprosyn
Relevance
Relafen
Fed up
Feldene
Lack of skill
Flexeril
Lethargic
Lortab
White tornado
Toradol
Crying
Tylenol
Craving
Carisoprodol
Rise and fall
Methocarbamol
Droll
Daypro
Vulcan
Voltaren
Silver lining
Elavil
Drizzle
Trilisate
Chloroform
Chlorzoxazone
Stupor
Pamelor
Desperate
Desipramine

Side Effects May Include:

Megeen R. Mulholland

Abnormal physical movements,
agitation,
anxiety,
black tongue,
blurred vision,
breast enlargement,
coma,
confusion,
constipation,
decreased breathing,
delusions,
diarrhea,
difficult or frequent urination,
difficulty in speech,
disorientation,
disturbed concentration,
dizziness on getting up,
double vision,
dream abnormalities,
drowsiness,
dry mouth,
excitement,
fainting,
fatigue,
hair loss,
hallucinations,
headache,
heart attack,
hiccups,
high fever,
high or low blood sugar,

hives,
impotence,
inability to sleep,
increased perspiration,
inflammation of the mouth,
irregular heartbeat,
lack of coordination,
loss of appetite,
mental clouding,
mood changes,
nausea,
numbness,
peptic ulcer,
rapid heart beat,
rash,
restlessness,
ringing in ears,
sedation,
sensitivity to light,
shortness of breath,
stomach upset,
stroke,
temporary paralysis,
thirst,
tingling,
tremors,
vertigo
vomiting,
weakness,
weight gain
or loss.

Transference

Beth Schorr Jaffe

I had been in therapy with Dr. Rocen for six months. At thirty-five years old I was the mother of two, and married to a loving and generous man. Loving, in that he wanted me to be relieved of my emotional turmoil, and generous, in that he was willing to pay the "Top Doc" his top price for treating me. Yet after all these months, I was not feeling better. The symptoms that presented when I first arrived at the psychiatrist's office had all but disappeared, but something new, unexpected, had erupted. The pain of it was dulled by the overall chill that froze my freedom to reason. But it immediately became the core of my therapy for many years to come. This day I became fully exposed. Like the random way I had dressed, my thoughts, too, were haphazard.

"Tell me about your fear of losing me," Dr. Rocen said. "Maybe there's a part of you that still doesn't trust me."

I felt the rise of heat from my legs up through to my chest. "No. Don't ever say that. I trust you completely." Feeling so strictly supervised, his ability to insinuate disloyalty made me painfully uncomfortable; burning me like the instigating sun of July in New York.

My conversation with Dr. Rocen continued. I looked down at my feet that were tapping alternately. "Maybe because this is your domain, I can't foresee what you will do with me in the name of therapy. Basically, you have full control here and I'm at your mercy."

"It's true that this is my office and I can do almost whatever I choose. But I wouldn't do anything that would hurt you."

"All right, all right," I steeled myself. "I'll tell you what's been going on." I took a deep breath. "This is so embarrassing, but I trust you, so I'll tell you."

"Good."

Another deep breath, and closing my eyes, "I, much too often, spend an inordinate amount of time worrying about the day when I will have to stop coming here to speak with you." I opened my eyes to blurt out a preconfession attempt to ensure forgiveness, "I'm sorry to burden you with this. It must be a nuisance. But it's a real threat to me."

"Go ahead."

"I depend on you for more than I have a right to. I depend on you to fill up the gaps in my life. I don't know where to go when I leave here. I dread having to face the day when I won't be your patient anymore. Giving up my time slot, I would think you have replaced me, and wouldn't want to care for me anymore if I had to come back." Hard as I tried to sit up straight and project this courageous confrontation, the real issue to be discussed lay in hiding, still.

Dr. Rocen waited. I continued, "I have let myself do the most awful thing and now if I tell you, you'll be so mad at me I won't be able to live." I wondered how my two perfectly affectless parents had raised such an animated child.

"Let me decide what makes me angry. At least give me control over my own reactions. Tell me what you've done." Fool he was to be so calm, I thought. I had such a shock for him.

I opened my eyes wide and tried to see his entire face and body in one view. After a few seconds I realized I was floating somewhere.

"You're off somewhere. You want to come back to the session? It will be over soon. I don't want you to go home feeling this way. Tell me what it is." His eyes stayed fixed, not blinking behind his glasses.

"Okay, okay. Dr. Rocen, I think I'm in love with you." I waited for the Love Guard to break through the door and remove me at once.

The doctor tilted his head to the side and let his lip turn ever so slightly upward. "Go on."

"I know you are very rigid about our work. That you won't stand for this kind of acting out. I don't know what to do." I started to cry.

The doctor scooted his chair a few inches closer to me and leaned forward to bring himself closer still. He pushed his glasses up to his eyes and spoke through my crying.

"Listen to me. I am very, very happy you told me this. That you were able to and that you trust me. This is very important stuff."

Dr. Rocen coughed and placed his hands fingertip to fingertip under his chin. "I think it is very important that you shared that with me. You have begun to develop a healthy transference with me. Do you know what I mean by that?"

I looked at him like he was the most sensitive and lovable man on earth. I couldn't wait to hear what I had said that was so healthy. "But I feel like I've ruined everything." I smiled at him. "What do you mean by healthy?"

"First of all, let me assure you that you have not ruined anything. Transference is an unconscious process. You are starting to feel things toward me that are actually your feelings about someone else, someone who is very important to you. Probably most important to you. The thing for you to try to understand is that it has nothing to do with me or who I really am. Because you don't know who I really am." He looked at me, waiting for some sign of cognition. "Do you get it?"

I looked back at him as though he was the one who was out of his mind. "You have got to be kidding. I don't think you're someone else. This is the way I feel about you." I watched his face.

Staring at him trancelike, I was aware that I wasn't speaking. I was locked in the stare he returned, absorbed at how large his seated body was; how his legs seemed to be the long branches of a tree falling in toward himself. I noticed him checking the time, and suddenly realized that my session was going on without me. I tried frantically to pull up something to say, and rushed in, "I think about you all the time. I'm afraid you'll throw me out. I worry that my appointment will be canceled. It's just a horrible situation." Feeling the futility of my own pout, I smiled for him, to show him I was strong. "So what do you think, Doc?"

The doctor sighed, and smiled a sweet, small smile. "I think you want me to worry about you. And why are you afraid that I'll cancel your appointments?"

"Well, what kind of doctor would you be if you didn't worry about your patients? Of course I want you to worry about me."

"Let's say I'm concerned. I care. But I don't spend all my time worrying about you."

"Do you ever worry about me? Would that be too much to ask? Would that be inappropriate?" I raised my voice. "Aren't you still my psychiatrist after we leave this space?"

"Are you angry with me?" he asked, smiling.

"No! I would never get angry with you."

"Don't you think that would be unnatural, never getting angry with me?"

"I think this whole relationship is unnatural." Here we go again. "How?"

"How? You know how. I tell you every intimate detail of my life and I'm not allowed to know you. You are in my life without any history. And not just for forty-five minutes, twice a week. That's what I'm trying to tell you."

He took a deep breath and replied, "Of all the people in your life, I am certainly one of the least important."

My shoulders started to twist side to side, rocking my bottom on the couch. "How on earth can you say that! You are not the least important person in my life—you are the only person. I live from session to session." I wanted to shake him into reality.

I hadn't meant to become so melodramatic. He waited, perhaps giving me a chance to compose myself. Watching me slip my wedding band off and on my finger, he said, "That was an honest display of negative feelings toward me. And you see I'm still here, same as before."

I slumped back, becoming mute, giving him a chance to make his point. "How angry you must really be to know I'm not as flexible as you would want me to be. Human. Not perfect."

"Now you're angry with me," I said.

"No. You're angry. You try so hard not to feel anything negative about me. Do you think our relationship is so tenuous that you can never disagree with me or oppose me in any way? Is that how you are with other people? Best behavior—good little girl?"

"You are not other people. You are the most important person. If I lost you I would have nothing." I folded my arms and hung my head.

"You are not going to lose me. Why won't you believe me? I only ask you to let other people in your life. You have a life out there, and I am not part of that. I will never be part of that. Never."

Never? He looked thoughtful, squinting his eyes and holding his lips tightly closed. I sighed and smiled; he didn't move a muscle.

He closed his file and stood to signal the end of our time. I sat quietly, then turned my face toward him, opening my eyes wide. I hoped he found them beautiful.

Consult

Mary Damon Peltier

When
I lay on the floor in his office,
he thought I was a fallen woman
offering myself:
provocative, brazen,
rather than broken
and present in the only way possible.

Suffering,
spread out before his eyes,
a messy picnic on the carpet,
I expected him to see me,
to be a scientist, a healer,
while professing his shock,
he was all eyes, all appetite.

Why Have You Come
to My Office Today?
Why Have You Come to the Hospital?

Mary Damon Peltier

If you know what you want,
you can't have it.
If you don't know what you want,
I can't help you.

Stop crying.

Why do you think you have
this ungovernable rage?

Do you think the rules don't apply to you?
Do you think you're better than everyone else?

Sarcasm has no place in the therapeutic environment.

A woman who can say what she wants
needs no help.
Others more needy
Others more grateful
would be happy to take your place.

My Last Freudian

Kake Huck

That's my last Freudian hanging in my head.
Balding, coy, surrounded by dark wood and
pricey art, the slow and glistening river making
sluggish halos through the glass behind his head,
he sits in careful colloquy with ancient voices,
staring at my angry snarl and frightened eyes,
telling me my bright refusal to be filmed
reveals a rebel's soul.

"If you don't want my skill, why don't you leave?"
he argues halfway through the second hundred
dollar session. His fingers twined, his tone like iron
swaddled in wet silk, his heavy body artfully relaxed in leather,
he offers me a different kind of freedom, thinking
in my weeping madness I will choose a
knowing father's glance.

He never billed me for the last half hour.

Fragments

Kake Huck

Don't make jokes:
they show you don't fully understand
the seriousness of your situation.

Don't drop names:
if you mention Laing or Karen Horney
it merely proves your need
to dominate the doctor.

Don't talk god to your cognitivist:
your superstition is her symptom.

Don't whine about method:
even rattles and chicken bones
can work.

And don't confuse your therapist
with your lover:
sometimes a cigar
is only
a cigar.

Misinterpreting Body

Cathleen Calbert

As we begin another millennium, I am
   a veritable hysteric, "generalized anxiety"

having mushroomed into panic; electric fish
   swimming in my bloodstream sing

warnings of my own death, heart lurching
   in my chest, palms cold cod, throat closing,

so I'm off to Dr. Z, who wears velvet slippers
   in his lush office and seems half-asleep.

He reassures me: "You don't need to worry."
   Good night, Dr. Z. Good night, Cathy.

With the help of his pills, my libido vanishes.
   My accommodating doctor promises

more chemicals to counteract the side effects
   I'm feeling (not feeling). I tell him, "I don't

want anything else inside my body," though I do
   miss masturbating on rainy afternoons.

Now not even my own hand interests me
   as if it's a boring date, whose talk is tiring.

At least, those eels no longer circle my spine.
   Basically, I'm okay, but I keep thinking:

If the mind believes it's misinterpreting body,
   how can anyone trust anything?

Dr. Abe's Psychotherapy

Shira Dentz

I.
A whale of a man
greets me at the door of his penthouse apartment.
Very friendly. Not the medicine man in his opaque box.
My mind wobbles.

The room is fashioned according to Freud,
lover of archeology and the primitive:
oil paintings, subdued olive couch,
two handsome leather recliners.
Totems from different countries,
a few plants.
Nothing truly rare, unusual or exotic,
but a pie-smell,
the innards of fantasy.

He recounts what he's been told me of me—
including, you're a *poetess.*

Points to three framed pictures
he drew in college.
Pale-yellow, black abstracts.

Taking three-quarters of the wall,
a woman's torso with flowing breasts,
blue and gold, coat of thin skins.
A gift, he says, *from the painter,*
a former patient.

The woods are in here too.
The cork lining the backside of the door

still has the nooks and crannies of a tree;
covering the wall beside the door,
the sallow cork of a bulletin board.
Anaesthesia-like,
the stem of our voices.

II

Before leaving the first session I ask
the sixty-year-old therapist;
a president of the psychoanalytic division of the A.P.A.,
of the New York society of clinical psychologists,
of a postdoctoral psychoanalytic program;

*Do you like me, I mean, do you have the feeling
you want to work with me?*
His response is wise: *Let me ask you this,
if I told you no, would you believe me?*

I liked the riddle approach.

I leave him on an exclamation mark: he's convinced
I know more of the true and real than I think,
and that he can convince me.
I smile like I have a lollipop.

Later,
he'd claim I made everything up.

III

At twenty-one I want to look androgynous,
stuff my femaleness out of sight:

for my first visit to a male psychologist,
wear a handmade maroon V-neck sweater
knitted by my best friend's mother,
and my own mother's gray trousers and blazer,
several sizes too big.

Dr. Abe's fingers pour downward: hair bristles
of a basting brush,
bent at the knuckles, ready to spread.

Five years later I watch
his lizard tongue flicker
at the curb of my mouth,
into which it disappears.
Tucked in so wide a man
was such a narrow tongue

He says *you think I'm doing this for you, but really*
I'm doing this for me.
Ten years later he swears:
You think this happened with me, but really
it was someone else,
for god's sake.

(These sections are excerpted from a longer sequence poem.)

Going Out

Catherine Turnbull

She told her first psychiatrist
she was too sick for words—unable,
even, to read the paper.

He gave her a book. Said, *Take notes
on the first chapter.* He said,
*You're a smart woman, why didn't you
become a lawyer?*
Why didn't you go to Dartmouth?

And in my heart, she tells him
Because Dartmouth
didn't admit women
until 1972.

Instead, she drove home
and put her head in a plastic bag
to see if she could stand
to suffocate.

When I phoned that psychiatrist
to say my mother got in the car,
sometimes, after wine, to practice
running the engine in a closed garage,
he asked me, *You mean,*
for the purpose of going out?

Therapy Session

Sharon Carter

The action of neuronal machinery in the therapist's brain is having an indirect . . . effect on the neuronal machinery in the patient's brain. (*A. J. Psychiatry* 155: 4 1998)

I think I'm inside out, but maybe
I'm just outside in.
If my brain connects to eyes
and ears,
is my outside really inside
or the other way about?
If you change my mind
with input, did your inside
travel outside
create neurotransmitters
somewhere within?
When I blush throughout
the session
did your speech transform
my thoughts into understanding
through my skin?
If you think, *therefore I am,*
how will I separate who is outside
from whom I think resides within?
If I'm allowed to choose
what happens, you know
I'll pick the status quo: remain
bewildered and inside-out,
rather than a savvy, outside-in.

Just One Question Doctor—
About My Termination

Beth Schorr Jaffe

Let me sit on your knee,
braid my hair
and tell me how lovely I am,
as I remind you of the girl
I thought I used to be.

And you remember, I know,
every word I've said,
so you'll remember I told you
a shot pierced my heart.

I tried to take doll's legs
and stuff the opening,
Twist limbs into knots,
Keep it all in,
though no child's toy could.

You tried to understand,
arrest the bleeding,
but could say nothing
to heal,
nothing to coax me
off this warm lap.

The arrowhead bore
front to back,
wound so deep,
Your mind adjusts to red
for me as I try

to smooth your face.
You wave your words
at me: Get well,
be graceful, proud of the woman
you are now.

I cower and stroke
your long hands.

If I smile
and promise to stop bleeding,
if I promise to stop hurting,
stop caring,
will you promise to be there?

The Story of My Therapy

Sondra Zeidenstein

All I know is I came to her composed.
I'd made it to 44 on my own.
I sat myself down in her tiny room
and said, *I'm lonely.*
I'm surrounded by people who love me
and I'm lonely. All I know is
the cream-colored Naugahyde chair
she sat in, for fifteen years,
her eyes never moving from my face,
and the emergence, slow
as a glacier thawing,
of an ache in my breastbone,
and slow, as a little girl's growing,
my willingness to feel it.
Sometimes I had to turn away,
unstick my eyes from her eyes' vigilance,
find relief in the blank-eyed mask on her wall,
in the glow of shut blinds.
Sometimes, years later, when pain
sharpened to a killing ache in my throat,
I was able to look in her eyes
and say *It hurts me to speak.*
I can't say how any of this happened,
though now, at 66, I look back
at the really small room where she sat,
eating, in a vacated hour, her hummus sandwich
reading Kabbalah or Revelations,
and I can see she is holding me,
a gentle, stubborn, fearless, uncompromising embrace—
while the breath I've been holding—
like a baby turning blue, forgetting the rhythm begun at birth—
the breath comes back into my body.

III: HOPE

Mrs. Gould

Mindy Lewis

1991 was a growth year. After bouncing about in the working world I'd settled into a job as graphic designer for a group of magazines; no small accomplishment. I had a good rapport with my colleagues, and my first open studio exhibition of paintings had been a success. The stigma left from my hospitalization—comprising two and a half years of my adolescence—had eroded into such a thin crust that only the occasional bout of hypersensitivity or defensiveness threatened to give me away. One day I looked around my office—really a cubicle—and in so doing took a metaphorical look at my life. Stacks of magazines I had designed were piled on shelves; photos of friends and my new boyfriend smiled at me from the bulletin board; color Xeroxes of my paintings were tacked up in neat rows. My Rolodex was filling with names of photographers, illustrators, type houses. When friends asked my mother, "What's your daughter doing?" she could finally say "working" instead of uncomfortably mouthing "freelancing"—her euphemism for struggling.

Basking in the realization of how far I'd come, I thought of those people who had supported and encouraged me. I remembered Mrs. Gould, who had taught our high school English class inside the New York State Psychiatric Institute. A bright spot in our drab days, clothed in all the color and culture of the world, she drew us out of our silences, loving our energy and irreverence, hating whatever caused us pain.

Was she still alive? A friend from the hospital had mentioned her a year or so earlier, but I'd been too busy to follow up. He'd mentioned she was no longer living with her husband and now had her own apartment in Greenwich Village. I called information; she was listed. I dialed, and after a few rings a throaty voice said hello. That familiar voice that used to recite Old English verse, making it sound fresh and juicy; infusing it with her delight, managing to gather the attention of the handful of distracted, rebellious, depressed, or agitated adolescents in her charge. Only now that voice sounded as chipped as one of my grandmother's china teacups.

"Mrs. Gould?" I could hardly get the words out. "Is this Shirley Gould?"

"Yes. Who is this?" She exhaled impatiently, wanting to get past the unnecessary formalities to the essentials; no time to waste. I'd forgotten this aspect of her personality. Let's get on to the important stuff: Shakespeare, Lorca, Tolstoy.

"Mindy Lewis, from P.I. Do you remember me?"

"Do I remember you? How could I ever forget you? How are you, darling? Is everything all right?" Concern tinged her words.

I assured her that all was well, that I was calling from work. "What work?" she demanded. "Tell me about your job." I briefly described what I was doing.

"And how are you? Tell me all about Mindy . . . what your life is like, who you are now."

I told her a little of my recent news and promised to send her a letter going into greater detail. Then I asked about her. Was she still teaching? She told me she'd stopped teaching at P.I. when they'd done away with the adolescent unit; she then taught at Bellevue for several years but had recently retired. "It wasn't like P.I., darling. It was heartbreaking. The kids just didn't stay long enough to make any difference, and the bureaucracy . . . very frustrating."

Hesitantly I asked about her husband. "Did Mr. Gould pass away?"

"Good Lord, no! He's very much alive. We're divorced."

"Oh, I'm sorry," I said in my best condolence tone.

Her throaty laugh blew away my apprehensions. "Don't be silly! Leaving him was the best thing I ever did! I wish I hadn't waited so long."

Mrs. Gould had always spoken proudly and lovingly about her children; I searched my memory to remember her saying anything in reference to her husband, a well-known conductor, aside from brief references. Yes, yes, he was famous; he traveled frequently. Then, waving her hand in the air, bangles jangling, she'd signal us to get down to work, and the reading and discussion and essay writing would begin. If we were lazy or didn't want to work, Mrs. Gould would push and prod our intellects to their feet, and together we'd pull meaning out of our shared experience.

Our fearless leader did not shy away from difficult subject matter; denial was not her style. One day we read aloud and discussed Dorothy Parker's poem, "Resumé": *Razors pain you; Rivers are damp; Acids stain you; And drugs cause cramp. Guns aren't lawful; Nooses give; Gas smells awful; You might as well live.* In this, one of many instances in Mrs. Gould's class, I shivered with the recognition that writers were able to express thoughts and emotions I knew well, but did not yet feel empowered to say.

"Thank you so much for calling me, for remembering me after so many years," Mrs. Gould now said.

"I never forgot you," I answered. How could I forget her, smelling of rose and musk, welcoming us into her classroom. As her motley crew shuffled in, she always asked each of us how we were, her enthusiastic interest an antidote to our beleaguered bafflement. In her class, we were considered whole, healthy, and entirely welcome.

She'd been a true ally, coming closest to an experience of unconditional love. Tough love, at times; demanding that we come out of our shells and join her and each other in experiencing literature. But always with humor, never to the point of invasion. If I wasn't feeling well and my headache or anxiety or depression kept me from participating, I was allowed to put my head down and rest. Passing my desk, she'd stroke my hair from my face, or take my chin in her hand and look into my eyes. If I was fuming, she'd challenge me to express it in words, then laugh at my string of obscenities. "I know how you feel, darling; I've had days like that myself! Now what about Dostoyevsky? Let's talk about rage as expressed in *Notes from the Underground.* Not up to it? Okay, anybody else?"

Together we experienced Lady Macbeth's hand washing, Hamlet's indecision, Robert Frost's musings, Kafka's alienation, Emily Dickinson's longing, Chaucer's sensuous appreciation of winter melting into spring. The full spectrum of human experience, which we had just begun to explore in our young lives. But above all else, we felt her commitment to us, her "brilliant children," and her belief that the intelligence and spirit of her group of adolescents on the fifth floor was worth more than all the psychiatrists in the world.

Although she would never undermine the authority of the doctors and encouraged us to talk out our issues in therapy, when a psychiatrist took an unjustly punitive stance, raising medication, denying privileges, or on occasion sending someone to Rockland, Mrs. Gould did not stifle her disapproval. When one of us was sent away after having been caught smoking a joint, Mrs. Gould exclaimed, "How idiotic! That's terribly unfair. Even my own children smoke marijuana occasionally." She was unswervingly on our side.

After exchanging clucks and chirps of delight at having rediscovered one another, we hung up. Immediately after we spoke I penned a letter, packed the envelope with magazines and photos of myself and my paintings, sealed it, and dropped it in the mailroom.

A week later her letter arrived. I recognized the same legible scrawl that used to decorate the margins of my assignments and essays, commenting and encouraging.

28 January, 1991

Dear, dear Mindy—

I have been reviewing those years—those terrible, terrible, wonderful years. I can still see you clearly—your sweet face, the grace of your movements, your wit and intellect. We were very bonded, weren't we? Never have I felt about any people the way I felt about that fifth floor class. No matter how much time passes—I never have to try to remember—it is in my consciousness always.

Thank you for taking the time to send those things to me— "This is where Mindy is today."

Thank you, thank you for calling me—Be good to yourself— I do love you dearly.

Shirley Bank Gould

I was surprised and moved. It had never occurred to me that we had impacted Mrs. Gould's life the same way that she had touched ours. Yet it confirmed something I'd always sensed: the love and commitment she emanated was not simply a routine part of her job. She delighted in us, and we felt it.

We spoke a few times after that. I suggested getting together for tea; she said that would be wonderful, but asked to wait until the cold weather passed. It was a particularly icy winter. The last time I phoned her, her racking coughing interrupted our conversation.

"Are you okay?" I asked when it subsided. "You don't sound good."

"What do you mean?" she asked. "How do you know?" Then she told me: cancer. This was why she postponed our visits. "You would not recognize me; I don't want you to see me this way." That was why her voice had that thin, brittle edge.

I held the phone and cried.

"Cry if you have to, darling, but don't be sad for me. I've had a wonderful life. I have marvelous children, and grandchildren. I've enjoyed my work, and my life. I wish the same for you."

One more time she told me she loved me, then we said goodbye.

Woman Knows It's Time
to Quit Therapy

Barbara Schmitz

I was brushing my teeth
staring at my face in the mirror,
and I just knew it.
Then at that moment.
That way I know some things
like I was once a beautiful woman,
now aging. I rinsed my mouth,
clicked my teeth together,
practiced a smile.

Today was my appointment
right before lunch. I would miss
my dark-eyed counselor who listened
gently as a grandfather,
supported my dream
like an American Dad,
heard my fears like a father confessor.

"I'm going," I said
at the end. He merely nodded.
"No, for good," I said.
"How do you know?" he asked.
"Like lightning all the way
to the ground in summer,"
I said. "September's breeze
following August still.
Like I knew with all my heart
who I should marry."
"So long," he said.

Simple Prayer

Anonymous

I was thirty-one, it was Christmas Eve, and I was checking into a psychiatric hospital in Southern California. A childhood trauma I'd run from my whole life had caught up with me. A friend said to me that morning, "You're not coping anymore. It's time to get some help."

Comfort and my first sense of hope came from two things the hospital provided. The first was the place itself. During the course of the insurance paperwork and the admission interview I became increasingly puzzled. A psychiatrist and I sat in a small cubicle: a desk, two chairs, one picture on the wall. It reminded me of the individual study rooms at the school where I got my bachelor's degree. The doctor took notes and listened as I spoke. I told him about the flashback of trauma I was reliving, had been reliving for weeks, and couldn't get clear of. He finished the paperwork and said, "It's good you came in. The nurse will show you to your room. I'll see you tomorrow."

I just sat. "Is there anything else?" he said.

"What is it you do here?"

"What do you mean?"

"I know you're going to treat me because I'm . . . having some trouble, but what else do you do? This whole building can't be just for that."

"This is a psychiatric hospital. We provide mental health care," he replied.

The concept of an entire building and staff devoted solely to how people felt in their heads was not computing.

"But don't you have an emergency room, like for someone with a broken leg?" Someone with real need is what I meant.

"No, we only handle psychiatric care here." I wanted to put this place into a frame of reference I understood: values involving productivity, or wounds that could be seen. I wanted to ask, "Do you take in laundry on the side?" But I didn't. It was 8 p.m. on Christmas Eve.

I was shown to my room. I unpacked my small suitcase (it's hard to figure out what to take to a mental hospital, especially when you're "not coping") and went to bed terrified.

At 6:30 the next morning I awoke. The door to the hall was closed. I got up and tiptoed over and pressed my ear against the door. I had hidden my wounds my whole life, and had no experience of receiving care. Standing there that morning, I was certain that when I opened the door, I would see a desert: a windswept empty landscape. In spite of the doctor's words, I didn't believe such a place could exist.

I opened the door. There was the maroon-gray carpet, the curving hall, the nurse's station. The hospital was real. Help might be real. A shard of hope broke from the shattered ceiling of heaven and fell into my hell.

The second blessing I received from my hospital stay was the food. Three times a day I padded into the cafeteria and chose whatever I liked from the steam table. I pushed my tray down the stainless steel counter, picking up little plates of salad, Jell-O, mashed potatoes, chocolate pudding. I pointed at roast beef or poached fish and a middle-aged woman wearing a hair net served my portions. When I got to the end of the counter, instead of paying the cashier—which staff and visitors had to do—I picked up my tray and headed to the beverage dispenser. One night I didn't like my fish, got back in line, chose a hamburger, and was not questioned.

I was a thirty-one-year-old woman with a college degree and a career, and it meant the world to me to be treated with dignity in a hospital cafeteria.

I received other gifts during my stay. A social worker helped me begin the paperwork to apply for disability. An attendant gave me a heating pad when my back went into spasm. My psychiatrist did not suggest drug treatment, but encouraged me to grieve the trauma and loss I had repressed for so long.

I've heard the horror stories. People given drugs when what they need to do is feel. People abused, molested. People disbelieved and disrespected. But for three weeks, when my life as I'd known it crumbled, I received comfort. In the afternoons, between cognitive therapy and assertiveness training, I'd wander into the Japanese garden in the center of the hospital rotunda. Sitting at the end of a gravel path, I'd watch slow, fat koi drift in the little pond. The frozen glacier of my grief began to soften and my tears fell.

Good mental health providers probably know they don't have the power to reach into hell and pull someone out, but maybe that's not the point. When doctors listen, when they offer a Kleenex or a hot meal, when society funds a hospital, maybe these acts are prayers. Maybe caregivers, driven by motives both selfish and selfless, are saying to God and to the devil, "We do not shoot our wounded. We can't always heal them, we sometimes misdiagnose them, and yes, we probably overmedicate them. But we don't load them onto a bus and push them over a cliff either." That may sound like thin comfort, but it wasn't to me. When I finally collapsed from a lifetime of pretending I was "fine," somebody took me in, gave me a meal and a bed, and asked nothing in return.

Clarity

Janet Ruth Heller

(For M. C.)

After I talk with you,
The heat wave lifts
And the air clears.
I can see every leaf
On the oaks and maples,
And, drifting from the cottonwood,
A million tiny parachutes.

Saying Goodbye

Pamela Malone

It's been a month since I left therapy and I still feel euphoric. I'm surprised. I'd been in therapy for almost six years, had grown attached to my therapist, and spent six months preparing to leave.

In fact, I was originally supposed to leave six months before my final departure date, but at the eleventh hour I had a feeling of panic, as well as a new "problem," and so I'd stayed.

Separation is a difficult thing, particularly when you have gone week after week, spilling out everything in your gut to someone who sits and listens, giving you her full attention for fifty solid minutes.

Someone whose every feature became part of your inner landscape; her warm brown eyes that genuinely showed concern, her beautiful soothing voice that always validated, guided, and helped me, not to mention her lap that looked so soft and motherly.

While therapy was often difficult, and I would sometimes come out of a session feeling worse than when I'd come in, I knew healing was taking place. Because I could feel the internal changes that began to positively affect my life.

When I told a good friend, who was also in therapy, that I was going to leave, her response was immediate. "Why would anyone *ever* want to leave therapy?"

A good question and one I had to ponder. Every week you can talk to a "friend" who knows everything about you, and will sit and listen, giving valuable nonjudgmental feedback and unconditional love. Who in their right mind, after finding this, would give it up? And why would *I*, who, before therapy, had had a hole inside needing to be filled?

The reason is because leaving therapy *is* therapy. Maybe even the most important part. How would I ever know that the therapy had worked, if I didn't leave it? Wasn't the whole point to prepare me to do so?

At my last session, I gave my therapist a poem I'd written in which I compared her to a tree with outstretched branches in which I, a bird with broken wings, had come to rest and heal. Now that my wings were healed, I was ready to fly. Because birds are supposed to fly. They're supposed to soar in the sky and feel the pleasure of their own wings, not stay in the safety and shade of a tree forever.

As the time drew closer, I said to my therapist, "I'm scared I'll fall off a cliff when I try to go out in the world by myself."

And she said, "But you're *already* in the world by yourself. And you're doing very well. Aren't you?"

This was true. I had reached the point where I was coming back to her and just reporting what I had done. And all she did was pat me on the back and say, "Job well done."

But still I had been fluttering above the tree. Yes, I was doing well. But only because I could come back and tell her about it. And she was always there like a safety net.

I expected to be depressed after leaving. Not because I wasn't ready to leave, but because separation is difficult. Especially separating from a good "friend" whom you know you won't see again.

Last summer, my college roommate visited briefly from California. I'd met her at Pennsylvania Station in time for a two-hour lunch, then she'd boarded a train that took her away. As I glimpsed her tall pretty face through the train window, our hands waving silently until her train fled into the dark tunnel, I felt grief. But it was only momentary. As I walked away from the station, her smile, her words, and that moment that we'd reconnected as friends came with me.

At my last therapy session, my therapist opened a beautifully decorated box that was filled with rocks and shells. She told me to take one. When I couldn't decide between a glossy green rock and a sculptured piece of white coral, she said to take both.

I took them home and keep them by the side of my bed. Sometimes, I'll think of therapy, and pick up the green rock. I'll feel its reassuring smoothness in my hand. But my therapist isn't in the rock. She's in me.

Keeping Our Distance

Lee Kottner

(For Christine Cameron Harris, December 30, 1997)

Midwife. Oracle. Inquisitor.
Guide into dark regions
and out again, saying things
no friend should say, can say
and remain a friend.
What are you?
For these three years
I have held you at arm's length
with both reluctance and need.
In another time
we might have been friends
of another kind.
I would have admired your paintings
played with your daughter
spoken other truths
as we sat over coffee
in my house or yours.

But you had something else to give me
besides unfettered friendship,
something both more and less:
tools as insubstantial as a cup of tea
but sharp as swords,
a view from a different mountain,
a bottomless vessel
I filled with rage and hope and tears.
We exchanged words—an imperfect medium

for love—so many millions of them,
and still I don't know
who you are.

Let's leave it so.
Even if I never see you again
I will come back to this room
this hour, this wellspring,
stand at this distance
and grow in your light.

Carol

Carol Barrett

Since we may never meet again let us say how our lives have
changed.

Anita Skeen

They called you my patient.
I called you my own name
and in that first hour of change
took your hand. They called me
unprofessional. It was not right
to move so fast. Touch is forbidden:
wait for the proper moment
when the patient is ready.
Clad in the arms of men
you had been waiting years.

I changed your chart,
rewrote medical opinion.
This was worse: county records
are private property. They discussed us
at long tables, analyzed my error
in rooms without sunlight,
their pointed words whittling
the air like chopsticks.
They were certain you would never
trust one of them again. You waited.

They hoped
I had gotten sufficient supervision,
instructed the co-therapist to take
charge. He began by asking your name,

place of birth, the length of your mother's
labor, sexual identity. You gave him
my name, all that was important.

The others waited their turns,
eyes vibrating the ashtrays. "Now what
is your problem?" he advanced. Our name
hit the one-way mirror like rivets.

He was commended for doing better.
They did not name us once,
scheduled you for individual treatment
with the primary supervisor.
He would handle the case well.

Before he was ready you left
for a new job. They insisted
this was moving too fast.
I celebrated alone. The co-therapist
was doing quite well now.
In the final hour our name holds
the chairs in place. A new intern
is assigned to write
our discharge summary.

Reflections for a Psychiatric Resident

Barbara Shooltz Kendzierski

I have a deep respect for psychiatry. You can effect tremendous healing in people's lives. And you are in a position to cause devastating pain and irreversible harm. People come to you vulnerable and frightened, finding themselves in a system they don't understand. To be trusted is a humbling privilege.

I suspect that what I need from you as a psychiatric patient is common to us all.

First, listen to me.

Listen to me as one human being to another. When I meet you in your office or in the hospital my first need is to be heard. Even if words have deserted me, if I sit in silence, if the most I can give is a shake of the head, I need to be heard.

Do not assume that you know my situation without having heard my story. I may surprise you.

No matter how logical, how rational, how clinically correct your approach may be, if you do not hear me first you only serve to reinforce the grim isolation of my emotional hell. I am not asking that you condone my actions or agree with my views. In fact, I may need just the opposite from you. But first, be with me.

I remember sitting in my hospital room feeling crushed by despair, pain, and fear. I could only gasp, "I'm drowning." My wonderful nurse nodded and said softly, "I can see that." That simple statement was a lifeline to me. She could have approached me rationally and pointed out that I was safely seated in a chair, in the hospital in no danger of drowning. All true but meaningless. Instead, first, she heard me.

Second, be an expert.

I need to be able to rely on you and to trust your clinical skills. Psychopharmacology, neurology, endocrinology . . . I know the demands on you to stay current in your field are intense. The stakes are high.

I may come to you believing that consultation with you is my last chance. I may not be thinking clearly. I may have difficulty making decisions. I may struggle to describe my experience or I may feel silenced. Take what I can give you and apply your clinical expertise on my behalf.

Third, respect me.

I may be hostile, uncommunicative, and even abusive. I may be unkempt and smelly. I may be tearful, demanding, and uncooperative. I may be arrogant. I may be silent. Look at me, through all of this, and see a fellow human being that deserves your respect.

At this point, my self-image is bleak. If you cannot look at me and see a person worthy of respect, you can only add to the depth and the blackness of my hell. You confirm my self-loathing. Respect me without regard for where I live, for what I have or have not achieved, for my education, or for any other condition of my life. Respect me because you see the inherent value of each unique human life, including mine.

If you believe in my value, your belief will be as powerful as any drug you will ever prescribe. There may be no known cure for my physical ills. But if you can reflect to me my human dignity, who knows? We may just begin to heal my spirit with a bond that embraces us both.

When Therapy Works

Maryhelen Snyder

When therapy works
there is an ocean
into which both people dive
unknowing. One of these
holds the faith. She
is the less brave
because she follows the other
who diving deeper and deeper
into darkness needs
to turn her face
and see someone there.

When therapy works
there is a body responding
as dolphins move
toward music; there
is the simple gift
of the other, saying:
I hear you;
You are
there.

When therapy works
it takes as long
as it takes.
The one who leads
(diving, and surfacing,
trembling, and laughing)
knows when it is time
to trust her body alone
in this darkness.

When that time comes
she will have felt all
the sea around her
as her mother.
She will carry her cradle
in her heart.

Afterword

This anthology of literary jewels written by women who have experienced mental illness has two very important functions. The first is that it represents a way for these women to connect with others who can give the kind of support, affirmation, care, and strength that only another person who has experienced the same events can furnish. Women naturally turn to each other in the midst of their distress to share stories, to borrow strength, and to endow their situations with meaning. They give name to a suffering that too often remains unspoken in therapy.

Moreover, this anthology speaks powerfully to professionals in conveying the complex world of mental illness to us that no DSM list of symptoms can. The understanding of certain experiences, such as the anguish of mental illness, can only be grasped fully by way of an inward appropriation of that experience. It cannot be approached by way of dispassionate description, such as those included in textbooks. Obviously we cannot all experience every human condition directly, but we can empathize through carefully selected examples of literary works. The language of the pieces in this collection has the power to awaken the total sensibility of professionals, students, and laypersons to new levels of consciousness.

Mental illness can be devastatingly frightening, and at other times can cause the sufferer to experience flights of ecstasy. Likewise, experiences with the mental health system can be abusive and dehumanizing, while for some, they can be healing and can save shattered lives. Regardless of the value placed on the illness time in their lives, two overarching themes emerge from the wonderful examples of women's experiences in this collection. The first theme tells us, "Hear me, I am a person!" The second cries, "Preserve my dignity, I am a human being!" Too frequently these spoken and unspoken pleas are not heeded by a system that is designed to label, control, medicate, and discharge.

The pronouncement comes, the diagnosis is conferred, and magically the woman patient is assigned a label that transforms her from *her* to *it*. These labels, once assigned in the context of mental illness, transform women into the entity that the label connotes—borderline, self-defeating, histrionic. The human behind these labels is lost; thus Kate Millet speaks of herself as "the discussed" because she has been transformed from human to patient by the simple act of receiving a diagnosis. In addition, when placed within the context of psychiatric diagnoses and milieu, these labels can illuminate how professionals tend to view a patient's actions as having their own origin in the condition (label) that is assigned to them upon diagnosis. Every word, every action takes meaning from the label because there is no longer a person there. We professionals have too often packaged women and others neatly into this or that category, robbing individuals of their humanity.

Once trapped by a bell jar, in a room with yellow wallpaper, no one listens. This sense of entrapment is devastating to patients, already limited by their own illness. To be further incapacitated by the culture of the systems we set up to treat those illnesses is unendurable. Gilman, Millett, and others describe this experience eloquently and convey its horror.

I have seen firsthand what such lack of power can do to persons in a psychiatric facility. The malignant emotional consequence associated with perceived loss of control, that feeling of being trapped, not only increases subjective suffering but impedes recovery. It strips one wholly of dignity. The lack of control over the minutest aspect of daily life, having received a label, the trauma of being removed from a familiar home environment, accompanied by the unsupportive atmosphere of an institution, presents people with a formidable task of adaptation. One has to find a way to sort out a sense of trust in people who are viewed as untrustworthy, including relatives who facilitated hospitalization. One also has to negotiate a relationship with institutional caregivers who are unknown entities, as well as find safety in situations that are perceived as unsafe and threatening. Finally, one must preserve a sense of control in situations that are unpredictable, and a sense of power in an environment fraught with uncertainty.

Thus the voices of these women entreat us: "Hear me, I am a person! Preserve my dignity, I am a human being!" And we, as professionals, educators, family, friends, and others must pay heed. It is, after all, so very little to ask.

Wanda K. Mohr, PhD, RN, FAAN
Associate Professor, Psychiatric Mental
Health Nursing, Indiana University/
Purdue University

WOMEN'S ENCOUNTERS WITH THE MENTAL HEALTH ESTABLISHMENT
Escaping the Yellow Wallpaper

_____ in hardbound at $39.95 (ISBN: 0-7890-1545-5)

_____ in softbound at $14.95 (ISBN: 0-7890-1546-3)

COST OF BOOKS_____

OUTSIDE USA/CANADA/
MEXICO: ADD 20%_____

POSTAGE & HANDLING_____
*(US: $4.00 for first book & $1.50
for each additional book)
Outside US: $5.00 for first book
& $2.00 for each additional book)*

SUBTOTAL_____

in Canada: add 7% GST_____

STATE TAX_____
*(NY, OH & MIN residents, please
add appropriate local sales tax)*

FINAL TOTAL_____
*(If paying in Canadian funds,
convert using the current
exchange rate, UNESCO
coupons welcome.)*

❏ **BILL ME LATER:** ($5 service charge will be added)
(Bill-me option is good on US/Canada/Mexico orders only;
not good to jobbers, wholesalers, or subscription agencies.)

❏ Check here if billing address is different from
shipping address and attach purchase order and
billing address information.

Signature_____

❏ **PAYMENT ENCLOSED: $**_____

❏ **PLEASE CHARGE TO MY CREDIT CARD.**

❏ Visa ❏ MasterCard ❏ AmEx ❏ Discover
❏ Diner's Club ❏ Eurocard ❏ JCB

Account # _____

Exp. Date_____

Signature_____

Prices in US dollars and subject to change without notice.

NAME_____

INSTITUTION_____

ADDRESS_____

CITY_____

STATE/ZIP_____

COUNTRY_____ COUNTY (NY residents only)_____

TEL_____ FAX_____

E-MAIL_____

May we use your e-mail address for confirmations and other types of information? ❏ Yes ❏ No
We appreciate receiving your e-mail address and fax number. Haworth would like to e-mail or fax special
discount offers to you, as a preferred customer. **We will never share, rent, or exchange your e-mail address
or fax number.** We regard such actions as an invasion of your privacy.

Order From Your Local Bookstore or Directly From

The Haworth Press, Inc.

10 Alice Street, Binghamton, New York 13904-1580 • USA

TELEPHONE: 1-800-HAWORTH (1-800-429-6784) / Outside US/Canada: (607) 722-5857

FAX: 1-800-895-0582 / Outside US/Canada: (607) 722-6362

E-mail: getinfo@haworthpressinc.com

PLEASE PHOTOCOPY THIS FORM FOR YOUR PERSONAL USE.

www.HaworthPress.com

BOF02